HYPERMODERN TIMES

Hypermodern Times

by
Gilles Lipovetsky

with
Sébastien Charles

translated by Andrew Brown

polity

The right of Gilles Lipovetsky to be identified as Author of this Work has been asserted in accordance with the UK Copyright, Designs and Patents Act 1988.

First published in 2005 by Polity Press

Polity Press
65 Bridge Street
Cambridge CB2 1UR, UK.

Polity Press
350 Main Street
Malden, MA 02148, USA

ISBN 0 7456 3421 4
ISBN 0 7456 3420 6 (pb)

24036099

A catalogue record for this book is available from the British Library.

Typeset in 11 on 13 pt Berling
by SNP Best-set Typesetter Ltd, Hong Kong

Printed and bound in Great Britain by TJ International Ltd, Padstow, Cornwall

For further information on Polity, visit our website:
www.polity.co.uk

Ouvrage publié avec le concours du Ministère français chargé de la culture – Centre National du Livre.
Published with the assistance of the French Ministry of Culture – National Centre for the Book.
This book is supported by the French Ministry for Foreign Affairs, as part of the Burgess programme headed for the French Embassy in London by the Institut Français du Royaume-Uni.
institut français

CONTENTS

FOREWORD

The work of Gilles Lipovetsky has had a great impact on the way we interpret modernity. In his first work, *L'Ère du vide* ([*The Age of Emptiness*], 1983), he set out the parameters of what was to become widely known in France as the 'individualist paradigm'. Ever since, he has continued to explore in detail the many various facets of the contemporary individual: the unprecedented reign of fashion, the metamorphoses of ethics, but also the new relations between the sexes, the explosion of luxury, and the changes within consumer society.

This attention to the most contemporary aspects of society might seem indulgent or complacent. Far from it: one of the virtues of his work is that, starting out from a minute description and archaeological analysis of the phenomena, he has gone beyond the traditional antagonism between ancients and moderns, between the euphoric fans and the Cassandra-like denigrators of modernity. He accepts neither the 'providentialist' model of a modernity that can always find a remedy for its ills within itself and turn its defects to advantage, nor the 'catastrophist' interpretation that thinks we are in a period of unbridled 'instrumental rationality', i.e. a rationality for which there are no ends but only means: neither of these views finds an unequivocal endorsement in his work.

The second modern revolution (or hypermodernity) that is happening before our eyes is by no means solely a matter of the disappearance of final ends. It is far from being a definitive victory of materialism and cynicism: indeed, quite the opposite – what we are witnessing is the revitalization of certain traditional feelings and values: a taste for sociability, voluntary work, moral indignation, and the value placed on love. These are all feelings and values that not only persist, but if need be become stronger, in a humanistic deepening of individualism. From this point of view, the interpretation of Gilles Lipovetsky might seem to be closer to the first 'optimistic' model of modernity, were it not for one major if subtle difference: it is in no way based on any invisible, providential mechanism, but endeavours to describe the phenomena of reconstitution and 'recycling' in the fine grain of their detail. There is no metaphysical wager here, but a falsifiable analysis of the phenomena (something to which neither the first nor the second model can lay claim).

This is the reason why this more complex and less one-sided interpretation of modernity does not lead to an idyllic vision of our present. This present is and remains paradoxical, both for its protagonists and for its interpreters: if hyperconsumption seems compatible with the values of humanism, it is certainly not the panacea that will deliver happiness to mankind. The hypercontemporary individual is more autonomous but also more fragile than ever, in proportion as the promises and demands that define him become ever vaster and more massive. Freedom, comfort, quality of life and higher life expectations do not blunt the tragedy of existence; they merely make its scandal crueller. In this book, written in collaboration with Sébastien Charles, Gilles Lipovetsky retraces his intellectual itinerary and the different stages his work has gone through; but he also makes a major contribution to his interpretation of the 'second modern revolution' by endeavouring for the first time to describe, in its most characteristic features, what 'hypermodernity' may hold in store for us – for better and for worse.

This work stems from several sessions that the Collège de Philosophie devoted to the work of Gilles Lipovetsky. Sébastien Charles, Professor of Philosophy at the University of Sherbrooke (Canada), oversaw and chaired the debates.

Pierre-Henri Tavoillot

PARADOXICAL INDIVIDUALISM
An Introduction to the Thought of Gilles Lipovetsky by Sébastien Charles

If we take the long-term view, condemning the present has probably been the most commonplace critical activity indulged in by writers, philosophers and poets ever since the dawn of time. Already, Plato was worrying about the loss of values and the emergence of an age of iron – his own – which no longer had much in common with the golden age of mythical times, endowed with every virtue. And if we are to believe Pliny the Elder, the exhausted world whose last moments he was sharing was being irreversibly led to its doom, as it was too corrupt to avoid it.

The theme of decadence or decline, taken up into a religious framework from an apocalyptic point of view, is not new, and everyone can easily find justifications that, in his or her eyes, adequately explain the quirks of their own period. Among the Ancients, who thought of history as cyclical, decline was ontologically written into the spokes of the wheel of fortune, and its arrival was seen as necessary. In the Christian world, the original Fall and the Last Judgement were the two beacons that illuminated a transitory present which was considered to be inessential. With the advent of modernity, there was a major break: it was not that the present was put back at the heart of everyone's preoccupations, but that the order of temporality was reversed, and the future, not the past, was made the place of the happiness to come and the end of suffering. This essential break in the history of humanity found expression in a discourse radically opposed to that of decadence, one which this time gloried in the conquests of science and laid out the conditions for the indefinite progress of which we were meant to be the heirs. Reason was to rule the world and create the conditions for peace, equity and justice.

This optimism, which was an essential characteristic of the philosophy of the Enlightenment and the scientism of the nineteenth century, is no longer in evidence. Following the catastrophes witnessed by the twentieth century, reason has lost any positive dimension and is now contested as an instrument of calculating and bureaucratic domination, and our relation to time, in particular the future, is now affected by this critique, even if some faint outline of the former optimism still persists, especially on the level of science and technology. Past and future have been discredited, and there is now a tendency to think that the present has become the essential point of reference for democratic individuals, since these people have definitively broken with the traditions that modernity has swept away, and turned their backs on a future that was far from rosy. The following text by Gilles Lipovetsky will show that, when it comes to the question of our relation to time, things are not so simple, on the one hand because the consecration of the present is not as obvious as is sometimes said, and on the other because the critiques made of it often miss the essential point.

One of the merits of the analyses that Gilles Lipovetsky has been putting forward for twenty years is that he moves away from those exaggerated judgements that are always too simplistic, envisaging as they do only one aspect of the situation: he can thus bring out the full complexity of reality and grasp the contradictions of which it is woven. In this sense, he is before all else a disciple of Tocqueville, who was the first to diagnose the emergence of individuals anxious to secure their personal happiness, nursing as they did limited ambitions: he also made it his task to highlight the numerous paradoxes that American democracy enabled him to judge for himself. Again like Tocqueville, Lipovetsky's analyses do not remain content with judgements that are over-hasty or subject to ideological diktats: they attempt, rather, following an empirical or inductive method, to start out from a long-term study of the facts and then propose an analytical schema that will interpret them and bring out their meaning. In this respect, each of his works is a critique of the simplistic conceptions of reality that are sometimes put forward, and constitutes an invitation to think through the phenomena of our world in a more complex way.

From Modernity to Postmodernity: Emerging from the Disciplinary World

The traditional analyses of the modern world, whether they are made by the Left or the Right, are generally based on a similar critique: the autonomy promised by the Enlightenment has ultimately led to a total alienation of the human world subjected to the terrible burden of the two scourges of modernity: technology and market liberalism. Not only has modernity failed to realize in concrete fashion the ideals of the Enlightenment that it had aspired to, but, in addition, instead of underwriting a transforming process of authentic liberation, it has given rise to an enterprise of real enslavement, both bureaucratic and disciplinary, exerted not only on bodies, but also on souls. Foucault was doubtless the thinker who pointed out most insistently this deviant aspect of modernity, namely discipline – a discipline whose final aim is more to control men than to liberate them. Discipline is a set of particular rules and techniques (hierarchical surveillance, normalizing punishments, investigation) whose effect is to produce normalized and standardized behaviour, to train individuals and to force them into an identical mould so as to optimize their productive faculties.

Now, at the very time when Foucault was still using the idea of discipline in its various guises as the principle of intelligibility of the real, Lipovetsky was announcing, in *L'Ère du vide* (1983), that we had entered a post-disciplinary society[1] which he called postmodernity; and, in *The Empire of Fashion* (published in French in 1987), he went on to say that modernity itself was not reducible to a mere disciplinary schema, if we took the trouble to envisage it from the point of view of that domain of the ephemeral *par excellence*, namely fashion. So it became a matter of moving away from Foucault's interpretation by showing that fashion, in allowing us to escape from the world of tradition and celebrate the present in its social aspects, had played an important role in the acquisition of autonomy; but it also meant taking a different tack from the logic of social distinctions as developed by Bourdieu, by showing that fashion could be conceptualized outside the schema of class struggle and hierarchical rivalry.

To be sure, the emergence of fashion is indissociable from competition between classes – between an aristocracy anxious to display its magnificence and a bourgeoisie eager to imitate it. But this does not exhaust the phenomenon, and does not explain why the aristocracy came round to investing so much weight in the order of appearances, or how the immobile order of tradition was rendered obsolete and overtaken by the interminable spiral of fantasy. We need to see this as a reaction to new landmarks, new aims and purposes, and not a mere social dialectic, a confrontation between people of different status. The problem with theories of distinction, such as Bourdieu's, is that they do not explain why competition, and struggles for prestige, between dominant social groups – struggles which are as old as the first human societies – could have formed the basis for an absolutely modern process, one without any historical precedent. Nor do they explain the origins of the motor of permanent innovation and the advent of personal autonomy in the realm of appearances. Class rivalries thus cannot constitute an explanation for the ceaseless variations of fashion.

The correct explanation turns out to be the one which consists in saying that:

fashion's constant shifts result above all from a new position and representation of the individual in relation to the collective whole. [. . .] Far from being an epiphenomenon, the consciousness of being an individual with a particular destiny, the will to express a unique identity, the cultural celebration of personal identity were 'productive forces', the very driving forces of the mutability of fashion. In order for the surge of frivolous changes to come about, a revolution was required in the *representation* of individual human beings and in their sense of self, upsetting traditional mentalities and values; we had to wait for the exaltation of human uniqueness and its complement, the social promotion of signs of personal difference.[2]

Indeed, by increasing the importance of the renewal of forms and the inconstancy of the realm of appearances, first and foremost on the level of clothing in the restricted circle of the aristocracy and then the bourgeoisie, fashion enabled the past to be dismissed and novelty to be promoted: now the individual could be affirmed over the collective, thanks to the way that taste became subjective and the reign of the ephemeral became systematic. It then becomes easy to understand how, within the economy of individual freedom, the frivolity of fashion should weigh equally with the modern cult of gravity and seriousness, thereby limiting itself to confirming the selfsame tendency to autonomy:

just as people have devoted themselves, in the modern West, to intensive exploitation of the material world and to the rationalization of productive tasks, through the fleeting nature of fashion they have asserted their power of initiative over the realm of appearances. In each case, human sovereignty and autonomy are affirmed, exercising their dominion over the natural world as they do over their own aesthetic décor. Proteus and Prometheus are of the same stock; although their paths are radically different, together they have inaugurated the unique adventure of Western modernity engaged on appropriating the facts of its history.[3]

Over and above the development of autonomy that it has underlain, fashion has also played a major role in leading modernity in a postmodern direction. For it was with the extension of the logic of fashion to the entire body of society, when society as a whole was restructured in accordance with the logic of seduction, of permanent renewal and marginal differentiation, that the postmodern world emerged. It is the age of consummate fashion, in which bureaucratic and democratic society is subject to the three essential components (ephemerality, seduction and marginal differentiation) of fashion, and presents itself as a superficial and frivolous society, which no longer imposes norms by discipline, but by choice, and the realm of spectacle.

With the spread of the logic of fashion to society in its entirety, we have entered the postmodern era, a very precise moment which sees the sphere of subjective autonomy widening, individual differences multiplying, regulative social principles being emptied of their transcendent substance, and any unity of lifestyles and opinions being dissolved. Hence, in *L'Ère du vide* in particular, this insistence on the central concept of *personalization*, which is used to explain a noteworthy shift in the dynamics of individualism that came into being with modernity. By enabling individuals to be freed from the world they belong to, and to become more autonomous (so that they need no longer follow a path laid down by tradition, but can all give themselves greater and greater margins of latitude), postmodernity has realized the ideals of the Enlightenment which modernity had merely proclaimed in juridical terms without giving them any effective scope.

However – and this is a major point which *L'Ère du vide* had already emphasized – this liberation from traditions, this access to real autonomy *vis-à-vis* the great structures of meaning, imply neither that all power over individuals has disappeared, nor that we have entered an ideal world without conflict or domination. Mechanisms of control have not vanished, they have adapted themselves by becoming less directive, by abandoning authoritarian strictures in favour of communication. People are no longer forbidden to smoke by legislative decree: instead, they are made aware of the disastrous consequences of nicotine on their health and their life expectancy. 'This is how the process of personalisation works: it is a new way for society to organize itself and find its bearings, a new way of managing people's behaviour, no longer by a tyrannical attention to detail but by exercising the least constraint and encouraging the greatest degree of private choice, the least coercion and the greatest degree of understanding possible.'[4]

It is clear that in no way does Gilles Lipovetsky tone down the role of negativity in the portrait he draws of postmodernity: rather, he wants to give a different meaning to this same postmodernity by suggesting that we no longer think of it as something simple but as a two-sided phenomenon. Basically, we need to realize that postmodernity presents itself as a paradox, and that two kinds of logic coexist intimately within it: one which favours autonomy, and one which increases dependency. The important thing is to grasp clearly that it is the very logic of individualism and the disintegration of the traditional structures of normalization that produces phenomena as completely different as self-control and individual apathy, Promethean over-activity and total lack of willpower. People are made more responsible for themselves, on the one hand, but are more freed from rules and regulations, on the other. The essence of individualism is indeed paradox. Faced with the destructuring of social controls, individuals, in a post-disciplinary context, have the choice of whether they accept their identities or not, whether they control themselves or let themselves go. Food provides us with the best example of this. As soon as social obligations, and in particular religious obligations affecting food (fasting, Lent, etc.), have disappeared, we see a rise in responsible individual behaviour (weight-watching, information on health, gymnastics) that sometimes borders on the pathological in its excessive degree of control (as in anorexia), *and* completely irresponsible attitudes that favour bulimia and the destructuring of one's mealtime rhythms. Our society, obsessed with slimness and dieting, is also a society of the obese and the overweight.

It is thus essential to realize that every increase in autonomy occurs at the expense of a new dependency, and that postmodern hedonism has two faces: it is destructuring and irresponsible for a certain number of individuals, prudent and responsible for the majority. Do we need any further proof? We need only think of the emancipation of moral behaviour, the other side of which has been a destructuring of the world of family and relationships, making relationships between people more complicated than in the past, when traditional norms imposed a place in the social order on everyone. Let's make no mistake about it: if Lipovetsky's work proposes a more complex and more ambiguous vision of postmodernity, if it rejects both the apocalyptic and the apologetic simplifications that are current in interpretations of our age, this is not so as merely to fall back into a blanket acceptance of our present, but to underline its essential paradoxes and to point out the parallel and complementary labour of both the positive and the negative.

From Postmodernity to Hypermodernity: From Enjoyment to Anguish

If the term 'postmodernity' is problematic in so far as it seems to indicate a major break in the history of modern individualism, it is still perfectly adequate as a pointer to a far from negligible change in perspective within this same history. To begin with, modernity envisaged itself as linked to two essential values – freedom and equality – and as promoting, in an unprecedented way, the autonomous individual who had broken away from the world of tradition. However, in the early modern period, the emergence of individualism went with an increase in the power of the state, with the result that this growth in the autonomy of the subject was truer in theory than in practice. Postmodernity represents the precise historical moment at which all the institutional brakes holding back individual emancipation disintegrated and vanished, thereby giving rise to the expression of individual desires, self-fulfilment and self-esteem. The great socializing structures have lost their authority, the great ideologies are no longer productive, historical projects no longer inspire people, the social field is no longer anything other than an extension of the private sphere: the age of emptiness has dawned, but 'without tragedy or apocalypse'.[5]

How are we to explain this change in the nature of modernity? Should we see it as a way of expressing in real terms those theoretical discourses that had celebrated the autonomy of the individual and the disappearance of the social structures that had previously framed it? While it is possible that this or that theoretical work may have played its part, and also possible that artistic modernism or the advent of psychology may have been influential, while increasing equality also had a certain impact, the essential cause lies elsewhere. In fact, it is first and foremost the phenomenon of mass consumption and the values it has put into circulation (a hedonistic and psychologistic culture) that are responsible for the shift from modernity to postmodernity, a transformation that can be dated to the second half of the twentieth century. Between 1880 and 1950, the first elements that would later explain the appearance of postmodernity were gradually being put into place, as a consequence of the increase in industrial production (Taylorization) and the greater availability of products rendered possible by developments in transport and communication, and as a consequence, too, of the appearance of the great mercantile techniques that characterize modern capitalism (marketing, supermarkets and department stores, the emergence of brand names, advertising). The logic of fashion then started to infiltrate, permanently and intimately, the world of production and mass consumption, and to make its power perceptible, even if it did not really contaminate society as a whole until the 1960s. It needs to be said that consumption, in this earliest phase of modern capitalism, still concerned the bourgeoisie alone.[6]

The second phase of consumption, beginning around
1950, was the moment at which production and mass consumption were no longer reserved uniquely to a privileged
class, at which individualism was emancipated from traditional norms, and a society emerged which was more and
more turned towards the present and the novelties it brought
in its train – a society more and more imbued with a logic
of seduction, taking the form of a hedonization of life acces-
sible to every different level of society. The aristocratic model
which had characterized the earliest ages of fashion tottered,
undermined as it was by hedonistic considerations. What followed was an extension, to all classes of society, of the liking
for novelty, the promotion of everything futile and frivolous,
the cult of personal development and well-being: in
short, the ideology of hedonistic individualism. Thus it
was that the model of postmodern society described by *L'Ère
du vide* emerged: in that work, society is better analysed
and explained by the idea of seduction than by notions
such as alienation or discipline. There are no longer any
models prescribed by social groups, but forms of behaviour
chosen and endorsed by individuals; no longer any norms
imposed without discussion, but a desire to seduce which
equally affects the public domain (the cult of transparency
and communication) and the private domain (the multiplication of individual discoveries and experiences). Hence
the appearance of Narcissus, the figurehead of *L'Ère du vide*,
a 'cool' individual, flexible, intensely hedonistic and libertarian at one and the same time. This is the euphoric and
emancipatory phase of individualism, experienced as a
disaffection with political ideologies, the waning of traditional norms, the cult of the present, and the emphasis on
individual hedonism. While the negative effects of this
divorce from the great collective structures of meaning
could already be felt – there is no liberation without a new
form of dependence – the fact remains that they have been
somewhat overshadowed. And yet the dual logic characteristic of postmodernity was already at work and exercising its
power.

Is the situation still as it was in *L'Ère du vide*? Can we consider the second phase of consumption as its terminal phase, one correlative with postmodernity? Are we still subject, as in the 1980s, to the same model of narcissistic individualism? Several signs suggest that we have entered the age of the 'hyper', characterized by hyperconsumption (the third phase of consumption), hypermodernity (which follows postmodernity), and hypernarcissism. Hyperconsumption is a consumption which absorbs and integrates greater and greater portions of social life, which functions less and less in accordance with the model of symbolic confrontations dear to Bourdieu, and which is, rather, arranged in such a way as to meet individual ends and criteria, according to an emotional and hedonistic logic which makes everyone consume first and foremost for their own pleasure rather than out of rivalry with others. Luxury itself, the essential element of social distinction, has entered the sphere of hyperconsumption since it is increasingly consumed for the satisfaction it procures – a sense of eternity in a world in thrall to the transience of things – and not for the status it enables one to flaunt. 'The quest for private pleasures has taken over from the demand that one flaunts one's status and win social recognition: the contemporary period is witnessing the establishment of a luxury of an unprecedented kind – an emotional, experiential, psychologized luxury, which replaces the theatricality of social display by the primacy accorded to sensations.'[7] Hypermodernity is a liberal society characterized by movement, fluidity and flexibility, detached as never before from the great structuring principles of modernity, which have been forced to adapt to the rhythm of hypermodernity so as not to disappear. Hypernarcissism is the name we can give to the epoch of a Narcissus who presents himself as mature, responsible, organized, efficient and flexible – one who is thereby quite different from the Narcissus of the postmodern years, who was intensely hedonistic and libertarian. 'Responsibility has replaced the festive utopia, and management has replaced protest: it is just as if we no longer recognized ourselves outside the domains of ethics and competitiveness, prudent regulations and professional success.'[8]

However, this time, the paradoxes of hypermodernity are blindingly obvious. Narcissus – mature? But he never stops invading the domains of childhood and adolescence, as if he refused to accept that he is now an adult. Narcissus – responsible? Can we really think so, when irresponsible modes of behaviour are growing ever more common, when declarations of intent are not put into practice? What can we say about those businesses which speak of codes of ethical behaviour while at the same time imposing mass redundancies because they have cooked their books, or those ship-owners who refer to the importance of respect for the environment while their own vessels carry out illegal oil-dumping, or of those building contractors who vaunt the quality of their products even though they will collapse at the slightest earthquake, or those drivers who are deemed to observe the Highway Code and who make phone calls while driving? Narcissus – efficient? Sure, but at the price of increasingly frequent psychosomatic disorders, depressions and burn-outs. Narcissus – a good manager? We might well doubt this when we observe the spiral of debt afflicting households. Narcissus – flexible? But on the social level he is more inclined to get extremely stroppy when the time comes for certain of the social benefits he has won to be revoked. The postmodern logic of social conquest has been replaced by a corporatist logic in which everyone defends their social advantages. And this is merely a sample of the paradoxes that characterize hypermodernity: the more responsible behaviour grows, the more irresponsibility increases in tandem. Hypermodern individuals are both better informed and more destructured, more adult and more unstable, less ideological and more in thrall to changing fashions, more open and more easy to influence, more critical and more superficial, more sceptical and less profound.

What has changed above all is the social climate and the relationship to the present. The disintegration of the world of tradition is experienced no longer as a form of emancipation but as a source of tension. It is fear which triumphs and bestrides the stage in the face of an uncertain future, a logic of globalization which acts independently of individuals, an exacerbated free-market competitiveness, a headlong development in the technologies of information, an increasingly precarious hold on one's job, and a worrying stagnation in the unemployment figures which [in France] continue to be high. Could you ever have imagined a twenty-year-old Narcissus taking to the streets in the 1960s to defend his pension, a good forty years before he would even be able to start drawing it? Something that might have appeared strange or shocking in a postmodern context now strikes us as perfectly normal. These days, Narcissus is gnawed by anxiety; fear has imposed itself on his pleasures, and anguish on his liberation. 'Self-obsession is these days demonstrated less in the fever of enjoyment than in the fear of disease and age, in the medicalization of life. Narcissus is less in love with himself than terrorized by daily life, and his own body as well as the social environment appear to him as aggressive.'[9] Everything worries and alarms him. At the international level, there is terrorism and its ravages, the logic of neo-liberalism and its effects on employment; at the local level, there is urban pollution and violence in the suburbs; at the personal level, a host of threats which render his physical and psychological equilibrium fragile. In short, the slogan is no longer 'Enjoy yourselves without hindrance!' [a slogan popular in 1968 – Tr.] but 'Be very afraid, however old you are'; and the Rémy Girard obsessed by disease and death in Denys Arcand's film *Les Invasions barbares* has logically replaced the dilettantish Rémy Girard of *The Decline of the American Empire*, fifteen years or so earlier.

The Loss of Meaning and the Complexity of the Present

If Narcissus is so worried, this is also because there is no longer any theoretical discourse that can reassure him. However frenziedly he consumes spirituality, he appears not the least bit more serene. The era of hyperconsumption and hypermodernity has sealed the decline of the great traditional structures of meaning, and their recuperation by the logic of fashion and consumption. Just like mass-produced objects and mass culture, ideological discourses have been taken over by the logic of fashion, even though they have always functioned in accordance with the logic of transcendence and permanence, and paid homage to the cult of sacrifice and devotion. Now, over the last two centuries, fashion was not able to impose itself in the social domain, since it was counteracted by ideologies that had the force of theologies. We left this period behind when eschatological convictions collapsed, as did the belief in an absolute truth of history. Transient enthusiasms have replaced faith; the frivolity of meaning has replaced the intransigence of systematic discourse; a casual attitude has replaced hard-line beliefs. In short: 'We are embarked on an interminable process of desacralization and desubstantialization of meaning that defines the reign of consummate fashion. This is how the gods die: not in a nihilist demoralization of the West and anguish over the loss of values, but in small jolts of meaning.'[10]

Systems of representation have become objects of consumption, and they are just as interchangeable as a car or a flat. Basically, what we are seeing here is a final demonstration of the modern secularization that was unable to develop fully in the past, being blocked as it was by all-embracing discourses that reinstated, via secular mediations, the idea of human submission to a higher principle – whereas the democratic ideal militated in favour of an autonomy of the human world, saturated on every level by individual aspirations. The system of fashion ends up making the happiness of individual persons sacred, and breaking up class solidarity and class consciousness in favour of personal demands and preoccupations. And to a certain extent, May 1968 can be seen as the application of the logic of fashion to Revolution. This event bears witness to the opposition between, on the one hand, an overt hedonistic individualism, and, on the other, various forms of social conservatism from a bygone age, which tended to restore hierarchical and authoritarian differences, in particular in the sexual domain.

> At the deepest level, what was at stake was a revolt aimed at harmonizing and unifying a culture with its own new basic principles. This was not a 'crisis of civilization', but a collective effort to draw society away from the rigid cultural norms of the past and give birth to a more supple, more varied, more individualistic society that would conform to the requirements of consummate fashion.[11]

We have reached the moment when the commercialization of lifestyles no longer encounters any structural, cultural or ideological resistances, and when the spheres of social and individual life are reorganized as a function of the logic of consumption. The first and final phase of consumption had led to the creation of the modern consumer by freeing him forcibly from tradition and fatally undermining the ideal of saving rather than spending money; the last phase has led to a boundless extension of the reign of consumption. That the logic of fashion and consumption has infiltrated wider and wider sectors of public and private life is evident. That individuals, deprived of any transcendent meaning, hold opinions which are less and less clear-cut and more and more fluctuating seems equally evident. But nothing permits us to say that the fickleness of these individuals is in itself to be condemned. Individuals are admittedly more mobile and more changeable in their opinions these days: is this necessarily a bad thing?

> Under the reign of total fashion, the mind is less firmly made up than before, but more receptive to criticism; it is less stable but more tolerant, less sure of itself but more open to difference, more receptive to evidence and to the arguments of others. To identify consummate fashion with an unparalleled process of standardization and depersonalization is to take a superficial view; in reality, consummate fashion is the driving force behind a more insistent questioning, a multiplication of

subjective viewpoints, a decrease in the similarity of small personal visions. The great ideological certainties are giving way [. . .] before subjective singularities that may not be very original, creative, or reflective but that are more numerous and more flexible than before.[12]

And in any case, were people any more original when religions and traditions produced a seamless homogeneity of collective beliefs?

On the one hand, the work of the Enlightenment is continuing: individuals are emerging from their minority and are more and more capable of freely examining what they are told, finding out about things and thinking for themselves in an ideological world where the immemorial norms of tradition have broken down and the terrorist systems of meaning no longer have any grip on people's minds. Intellectual authorities have not disappeared as a result; they merely exercise their influence differently, by making argument more important than the imposition of an opinion. Opinion exerts its power too, but its weight is more optional than definitive, and it helps people to make up their own minds and identities. But at the same time, nothing enables us to discriminate between information and disinformation: the craziest theories are welcomed with open arms and turned into best-sellers (we need only remember how the attacks of 11 September 2001 were attributed to the American secret services, not to mention all the conspiracy theories that have flourished ever since); an ever greater number of beliefs flourish in our cities, sects are recruiting more adherents than ever before, the sciences of the paranormal are enjoying a new credibility . . .

Is the Logic of Consumerism All-Powerful?

Every day the world of consumption appears to infiltrate our lives and modify our relationships with objects and human beings. In spite of this, and despite the critiques that have been made of it, no credible alternative model has yet been proposed. And once we move beyond a critical posture, it would be rare to find anyone who really wished to abolish it definitively. We are forced to the conclusion that its dominion is ceaselessly spreading: the principle of do-it-yourself, the quest for emotions and pleasures, the utilitarian calculus, the superficiality of the bonds between people – all seem to have contaminated society as a whole. Not even spirituality itself is exempt. Religion in its turn has started to follow the consumerist agenda: it has abandoned asceticism in favour of hedonism and a liking for parties; it has set the values of solidarity and love higher than those of contrition and contemplation. And the same is just as true in the case of family life, in our relation to ethics, politics or trades unions, or even in our relation to nature. Hyper-modernity really does function in accordance with the logic of the permanent recycling of the past: nothing seems to escape its grip.

If another example is needed, let us take the way that women have gained access to autonomy. People have raised the question of why certain traditional distinctions have persisted – as if the attempt to achieve equality had not been taken to its logical conclusion, namely, the merging of genders. But we need to understand that while certain social norms or traditional functions that used to be incumbent on women have been maintained, this is because they have been recycled by the logic of individualism: women have appropriated them with an eye to procuring more private happiness for themselves, and not because they constitute an archaic survival which, by feminist criteria, ought to be jettisoned.

If women still have a privileged relation to the domestic, sentimental or aesthetic spheres, this is not simply the result of social pressures but because these spheres are so arranged as not to get in the way of the principle of one's free possession of oneself: they function as vectors of private identity, meaning and power. The different paths followed by men and women are renegotiated from within individualist-democratic culture itself.[13]

In the world of hyperconsumption, even the housewife can be recycled . . .

Is the consumerist logic totally hegemonic, capable of absorbing and recycling everything in accordance with its own rationality? The functioning of the liberal world which generates more profits, more efficiency and more rationality seems to justify the fears of Heidegger, who denounced what was happening in technology: its inner meaning was being confiscated by a 'will to will', a dynamic of power feeding on itself, with no other aim than its own development. The will, which was initially impelled by the laudable desire to relieve humanity from its immemorial suffering, has gradually been transformed into a will to power, and its sole aim is to maintain its dominion over men and things: in the final analysis it produces the world we live in, obsessed as it is with technology and performance. This idea has recently been taken up by Taguieff: he shows that the logic of precipitate modernization has lost any real human purpose, and that technology has led to a decline in all values. These two aspects then lead directly to a form of neo-nihilism.

Yet we must not paint too black a picture of things: not everything can be reduced to pure consumption, and not everything is recyclable. Certain values proper to modernity, such as human rights, are not about to collapse in a welter of pure consumerism. Other values are also partly immune to the world of consumption – the desire for truth, or the importance of human relationships. While it is noteworthy that the obsession with brand names has invaded the intellectual world and led certain thinkers to succumb to the demands of marketing, the fact remains that intellectual honesty and the concern for truth continue to be the prerogative of the majority. In the final analysis, the desire to know has in most cases retained its superiority over the desire to please and to be recognized, and the slow rhythm of theoretical thought is not about to adapt to the extremely fast-moving rhythm of the society of the spectacle.

> Intellectuals are still the obstinate forgers of *meaning*. As such they are an old-fashioned species, far from ready to *rush through* their work in a shameless attempt to meet their deadlines. Perhaps it is intellectual work, being inevitably something done with craftsmanship and love, that will be most able, here and there, to offer the most stubborn resistance to frivolity, to the way the world is converted into spectacle.[14]

'Love': once the word has been uttered we realize that this is another domain that lies outside the sphere of interest, as, more generally, do all the relationship values which to a great extent comprise the full richness of our private lives. At the very moment when our relationship to the world of things and people seems to be essentially predatory in character, here is a domain which presents itself as functioning in a totally disinterested way. The reign of money is not the gravedigger of human affections: on the contrary, it is what endows it with its full legitimacy, as if we felt the need to rediscover a certain innocence in a world that is increasingly ruled by efficiency and rationality.

So nothing could be further from the truth than the belief that consumption rules absolutely. And nothing could be further from the truth than the belief that, by reducing individuals to the role of consumers, it favours social homogenization. The most important task is not to deplore the atomization of society but rather to rethink social reality in a hypermodern context when no ideological discourse makes sense any more, and when the disintegration of society has reached its peak. Of course, society is being reconstituted, but in a way that starts out uniquely from the singular desire of individuals. Individual atoms are far from averse to forming links, communicating, and coming together in associative movements, admittedly marked by egocentricity since their belonging is spontaneous, supple and selective, and at every point follows the logic of fashion. But are narcissistic groupings enough to make a democratic society and to promote a sense for values when consumption alone seems to be essential?

Ethics between Responsibility and Irresponsibility

Is our hypermodernity, characterized as it is by emotional consumption and individuals whose main anxiety is their health and their security, a sign of the increasing hold of barbarism on our societies? There are many who criticize our current state: in it they see only enfeebled souls, inner barbarity, the defeat of thought or the imperfection of the present. As if the nihilism in which Nietzsche foresaw Europe's future had indeed triumphed. And from one point of view this conclusion is not wrong: individualist hedonism, undermining the traditional institutions of social control and emptying the social arena of all transcendence, deprives a certain number of individuals of their reference points and encourages an unbridled individualism which seems to give free rein to any kind of pretentious verbiage. How can we ignore the proliferation of sects, which seduce otherwise well-educated individuals, or the return of the paranormal, when such phenomena had been discredited by modernity? Bayle and Fontenelle must be turning in their graves – but this will not modify in the slightest the hypermodern logic that keeps redeveloping and recycling the past.

But relativism is only one possible face of hypermodernity. We must also admit that human rights have never been viewed with such a high degree of consensus as today: the values of tolerance and respect for others have never been so strongly in evidence as now, and this has entailed a ubiquitous sense of revulsion against the gratuitous use of violence. And then, how can we ignore the fact that hypermodernity has been formed in tandem with an increasingly explicit ethical demand? We are all too often presented with a portrait of catastrophe, in which ethics has deserted the social arena and been replaced by cynicism or egotism: but we need to emphasize that, in the face of the threats engendered by technical and scientific development and the withering away of grand political projects, a strong need is currently being expressed for ethical regulation and codes of practice, whether on the social or economic level,[15] or even in the mass media. To be sure, ethical concerns are no longer experienced, as they were in the past, as following a logic of sacrificial duty, and they need to be seen as taking the form of a painless, optional morality, which works more in accordance with emotion than obligation or punishment, and has adapted itself to the new values of individualist autonomy.[16] But this post-moralist phase which characterizes today's societies does not entail the disappearance of all ethical values.

> At the same time as the priesthood of duty and the taboos of the Victorian era have become obsolete, new regulations have come into being, prohibitions have been re-established, values have been re-imposed, thereby producing the image of a society that is quite unrelated to the one described by all those who condemn its 'ubiquitous permissiveness'. Hymns to a sense of duty that could tear you apart are no longer heard in society, but moral behaviour has not collapsed into anarchy; well-being and pleasure are more widespread and important, but civil society is avid for order and moderation; subjective rights govern our culture, but 'everything is not permitted'.[17]

It is clear from all this that post-morality is not the same as immorality. There are three things that enable us to highlight the persistence of ethical ideals in an individualist context. First, the disappearance of an unconditional morality has not led in consequence to egotistic behaviour spreading to society as a whole, as is shown by the profusion of mutual aid and voluntary societies. Then, the relativism of values has not contributed to moral nihilism, since a hard core of essential democratic values has been preserved, and a strong consensus has been established around this core. Finally, the loss of traditional reference points has not created the social chaos that had been predicted, given that individual liberation, especially in the sexual domain, has not led to total anarchy in behaviour.

While all this is the case, the way that individuals have been made responsible for their own lives is merely one face of hypermodernity. We must not forget, too, that the dissolution of the frameworks that kept people in their place can produce the opposite effect. With the collapse of the great normative discourses on morality, we are witnessing unprecedented asocial phenomena that are all marked by an irresponsible individualism: ubiquitous cynicism, the rejection of effort and individual sacrifice, compulsive behaviour, drug trafficking and addiction, and gratuitous violence, especially against women in the suburbs. The reign of hedonism coincides only partially with the age of increased individual responsibility.

The Paradoxes of the Media Industry

While morality has not disappeared from the social arena, it is none the less still imposed from outside, by messages transmitted by the media, rather than being determined from within. It is true that moral norms are no longer decreed and imposed, as in the past, by the national spirit, the family or the churches, and that the landmarks provided by the traditional institutions are now meaningless and have had to be adapted to the logic of the ephemeral. It is also correct to say that our society, fascinated by all that is frivolous and superfluous, has entered its flexible and communicative period, characterized by the love of spectacle and the mutability of opinions and social formations. There is nothing very original in this remark, since the traditional critique of the world of the media, as voiced in particular by the Frankfurt School and the Situationists, consists in attributing to them an omnipotence that has helped to turn them into instruments of manipulation and alienation, totalitarian in essence, whose aim is the justification of the established order, and conformism and standardization among individuals. While we are forced to admit that the media do indeed play a nor-malizing role, and to agree that their grip on everyday life is far from negligible, we will still not jump to the hasty con-clusion that they have a power of unlimited mass homoge-nization. Indeed, the media can encourage this or that kind of behaviour on the part of the public, but they cannot impose it. One proof is the fact that a certain message may be hammered out again and again but still fail to produce the desired effect (we need only think of the anti-tobacco advertising campaigns, which seem not to have diminished the number of smokers perceptibly).

In spite of everything, can we not concede that the Situa-tionist critique has a considerable degree of legitimacy? Are we not completely saturated by messages from outside that condition and standardize our behaviour? But this conclusion ignores the positive effects of the logic of fashion, and of con-sumption, which have gradually made us indifferent to the messages of advertising and the objects produced by indus-try. This disaffection *vis-à-vis* the world of consumption has made possible in return a conquest of personal autonomy, by multiplying the opportunities for individual choice and the sources of information about products. Far from leading to the emergence of one-dimensional man, as Marcuse feared, the logic of consumption and fashion has encouraged the emergence of an individual who is more the master and pos-sessor of his own life, albeit basically unstable, without any deep-rooted attachments, and with a personality and tastes that are always fluctuating. And it is because he is so consti-tuted that he needs an ethics that is presented as spectacle – for this alone is able to move him and impel him to act. The media have been obliged to adopt the logic of fashion, to fall into line with the world of spectacle and superficiality, and to emphasize the seductiveness and entertainment value of their messages. They have thereby adapted themselves to the fact that personal reasoning and argument develop less and less by means of discussion between private individuals, and more and more by means of consumption and the seductive path-ways of information.

While the negative aspects of the media can be re-evaluated in terms of their relative power to exert a normalizing influence, we should also underline their positive aspects. After all, in the history of modern individualism, the media have played a major emancipatory role by spreading hedonistic and libertarian values throughout society as a whole. 'By making the right to individual autonomy sacred, by promoting a culture of relationships, by celebrating the love of the body, pleasure and private happiness, the media have been responsible for dissolving the force of traditions and the old watertight divisions between classes, and loosening strict codes of morality and the great political ideologies.'[18] Even more, by enabling people to gain access to increasingly diversified information and to different viewpoints, and by proposing a range of extremely varied choices, the media have enabled individuals to be granted a greater autonomy of thought and action while permitting them to make up their own minds on an ever-increasing number of phenomena.

On the political level, for instance, their formative role has been decisive. Rather than seeing them as responsible for the degradation of public debate, it would be better to view in more favourable terms their influence on the political maturity of an electorate less and less hidebound by ideological discourse or by the logic of class conflict, and more and more alert to the arguments put forward by competing political parties. And this can only contribute to democratic debate. Furthermore, our societies are characterized not by consensus but by a permanent discussion to which the media contribute to a great extent. Our societies, deprived of transcendent meaning or any universally recognized authority, are obliged to be the site of a permanent struggle between antagonistic discourses against a background of democratic stability, with freedom and equality constituting a common ideal basis – a basis that is, none the less, problematic, since these two principles (freedom and equality) are susceptible to opposite interpretations. So we are not in thrall to an era in which convictions and behaviour have perforce become rendered completely uniform. The homogenization of tastes and lifestyles does not lead to a consensual political and social life, since there are still conflicts – but they persist via an individ-ualistic pacification of the collective debate to which the media have contributed. One example is the fact that the controversial election of George W. Bush (2000) did not give rise to any bloodshed. We are no longer living through the era of great and bloody collective tragedies: but tragedy *is* still experienced, albeit in a more individual way, and the stresses and strains of life are increasing, while the future has never before appeared so threatening. Hypermodernity is the reign neither of absolute happiness, nor of total nihilism. In one sense, it is neither the accomplishment of the Enlightenment project, nor the confirmation of Nietzsche's dark predictions.

This defence of the realm of the mass media is meant merely to relativize the phenomena, and does not seek to conceal the negative aspects gnawing away at the system of the media in particular, and hypermodernity in general. It is obvious that by exacerbating individualism and assigning less and less importance to traditional discourses, hypermodern society is characterized by several features: indifference to the public good, the priority often granted to the present over the future, the rise of the interests of individuals and corporations, the disintegration of the sense of duty or debt towards the collectivity. These analyses, while restricted to the sphere of the media, can be just as critical, since the media too are affected by the dual logic characteristic of the hypermodern world, which makes all things ambiguous.

How could we ignore the negative effects of the media on culture and the public debate? They are supposed to inform us, but in fact they disinform us, in the interests either of sen-sationalism (the mass graves of Timisoara) or of vulgar poli-tics (think of the murky role played by the American channel Fox during the 2003 war in Iraq). Instead of raising the level of public debate, they transform politics into a spectacle. Rather than being the promoters of a high-quality culture, they swamp us with insipid variety shows, churn out more and more sports programmes, and broadcast anything 'cul-tural' as late as they possibly can (or cut it altogether). They are seen as favouring individual freedom and initiative, whereas consumers become increasingly dependent on them.

It is their job to shape a critical spirit able to pass judgement, but the logic of market forces means that thinking is often neglected in favour of emotion, and theory in favour of practical usefulness. Hence the vogue for philosophical works whose only hope of success lies in responding to personal anxieties and offering recipes for achieving happiness. 'It is not a passion for thinking which proves successful, but rather the demand for knowledge and information that have an immediate practical use.'[19] In their turn, the media succumb to the logic of hypermodernity and can encourage both responsible and irresponsible behaviour.

The future of hypermodernity will be played out here, in its capacity to enable the ethics of responsibility to win out over irresponsible behaviour. Irresponsible behaviour is not going to disappear of its own accord, since it is necessarily built into the logic of hypermodernity. In fact, it is the very mechanisms of democratic individualism which explain both the responsibility of one set of people and the irresponsibility of another – of those who prefer to pervert the autonomy they have inherited into pure egotism. The latter, anxious only about their own comfort and happiness, abandon the social realm for the private realm, and have a perfectly good conscience about doing so, since the traditional institutions that governed social behaviour, discredited by the advance of individualism, no longer play their normative role. But we should not exaggerate the extent of this phenomenon, either, since responsible behaviour is still a fact of current life. This is perhaps the most astonishing fact: the society of mass consumption, emotional and individualistic as it is, allows an adaptable spirit of responsibility to coexist with a spirit of irresponsibility incapable of resisting either external temptations or internal compulsions. The fact is that the binary logic of our societies will continue to increase, and everyone will become more and more responsible for themselves. Never has a society allowed individual autonomy and freedom such far-reaching expression; never has its destiny been so linked to the behaviour of those who comprise it.

The advantage of the binary vision that we find in the work of Lipovetsky is that it offers us, outside Marxist and liberal frameworks, another reading of the present in which the future of our democracies is open, and in which individual and collective responsibility is fully insisted on. Against the liberals, who think that liberalism alone can resolve the difficulties that it creates, Lipovetsky reminds us that the role of the market has its limits and that the invisible hand of providence supposed to regulate it from within needs a very visible pair of gloves if it is to be safeguarded against its excesses. Against the Marxists, who denounce the contradictions they discover within the logic of capitalism, and militate in favour of a classless society that will necessarily come about, Lipovetsky shows that the contradiction has been carried over into the very hearts of individuals, that symbolic struggles have diminished in intensity, and that the future is unpredictable because we need to build it, together, in the present. By facing up to the complexity of the present, and refusing to accept idealistic or over-pessimistic views of it, Lipovetsky puts forward an interpretation of our hypermodernity that seeks to be at once rationalistic and pragmatic, and in which a sense of responsibility is the cornerstone of the future of our democracies. Without any real sense of responsibility, virtuous declarations of intent devoid of any concrete effects will not be enough. We need to emphasize the importance of people's intelligence, mobilize institutions, and prepare our children to face the problems of the present and the future. Responsibility must be collective and must exert itself in every domain of power and knowledge, but it must also be individual, since in the final analysis it is up to us to accept the autonomy that modernity has bequeathed to us.

NOTES

1 On the relation to Foucault, see my interview with Gilles Lipovetsky published in *La Philosophie française en questions*:

entretiens avec Comte-Sponville, Conche, Ferry, Lipovetsky, Onfray, Rosset (Paris: Le Livre de poche, 2003).

2 Lipovetsky, *The Empire of Fashion: Dressing Modern Democracy*, tr. Catherine Porter (Princeton: Princeton University Press, 1994), p. 46.

3 Ibid., pp. 24–5 (translation slightly modified).

4 Lipovetsky, *L'Ère du vide: essais sur l'individualisme contemporain* (Paris: Gallimard, 1983; republished in collection 'Folios Essais'), p. 11.

5 Ibid., p. 16.

6 On all this, see Lipovetsky, 'La société d'hyperconsommation', *Le débat*, 124 (2003), pp. 74ff.

7 Lipovetsky, 'Luxe éternel, luxe émotionnel', in Gilles Lipovetsky and Elyette Roux, *Le Luxe éternel: de l'âge du sacré au temps des marques* (Paris: Gallimard, 'Le débat', 2003), pp. 60–1.

8 Lipovetsky, *L'Ère du vide*, pp. 316–17.

9 See Lipovetsky, 'Narcisse au piège de la postmodernité?', in *Métamorphoses de la culture libérale: ethique, médias, entreprise* (Montreal: Liber, 2002), p. 25.

10 Lipovetsky, *Empire of Fashion*, p. 206.

11 Ibid., p. 210. On Lipovetsky's reading of May 1968, see 'Changer la vie, ou l'irruption de l'individualisme transpolitique', *Pouvoirs*, 39 (1986), tr. as 'May '68 or The rise of transpolitical individualism', in Mark Lilla (ed.), *New French Thought: Political Philosophy* (Princeton, NJ: Princeton University Press, 1994).

12 Lipovetsky, *Empire of Fashion*, pp. 222–3.

13 Lipovetsky, *La Troisième Femme: permanence et révolution du féminin* (Paris: Gallimard, 1997), p. 13.

14 Lipovetsky, 'Monument interdit', *Le débat*, 4 (1980), p. 47.

15 On Lipovetsky's interpretation of business ethics, see his 'L'âme de l'entreprise: mythe ou réalité?', in *Métamorphoses de la culture libérale*, pp. 55–85.

16 Lipovetsky, 'Mort de la morale ou résurrection des valeurs?', in *Métamorphoses*, pp. 31–51.

17 Lipovetsky, *Le Crépuscule du devoir* (Paris: Gallimard, 1992), p. 51.

18 Lipovetsky, 'Faut-il brûler les médias?', in *Métamorphoses*, p. 93.

19 Ibid., p. 98.

TIME AGAINST TIME
Or The Hypermodern Society

Around the end of the 1970s, the notion of postmodernity emerged on to the intellectual scene, with the aim of describing the new cultural state of developed societies. First appearing in architectural discourse in reaction against the international style, it was rapidly taken up and used to designate, on the one hand, the shaking of the absolute foundations of rationality and the bankruptcy of the great ideologies of history and, on the other, the powerful dynamic of individualization and pluralization within our societies. Over and above the different interpretations put forward, the idea gained acceptance that we were dealing with a more diverse society, one with less compulsion and less laden with expectations of the future. The enthusiastic visions of historical progress were succeeded by narrower horizons, a temporality dominated by precariousness and ephemerality. Inseparably associated with the collapse of earlier heroic constructions of the future and the concomitant triumph of consumerist norms centred on living in the present, the postmodern period indicated the advent of an unprecedented social temporality marked by the primacy of the here-and-now.

The neologism 'postmodern' had one merit: that of bringing out a change of course, a profound reorganization in the way that advanced democratic societies worked, both socially and culturally. The dramatic rise in consumption and mass communication, the waning of authoritarian and disciplinary norms, the rising tide of individualism, the primary role now accorded to hedonism and psychologism, the loss of faith in a revolutionary future, the disaffection with political passions and militant positions: some name had indeed to be found for the formidable transformation that was being played out on the stage of opulent societies disburdened of the great futuristic utopias of modernity at its inception.

But at the same time, the expression 'postmodern' was ambiguous, clumsy, not to say loose. It was, of course, a modernity of a new kind that was taking shape, not any surpassing of modernity. Hence the legitimate hesitation that people showed with regard to the prefix 'post'. We can add this: twenty years ago, the concept 'postmodern' was a breath of fresh air, it suggested something new, a major change of direction. It now seems vaguely old-fashioned. The postmodern cycle unfolded under the sign of the 'cool' decompression of the social realm; these days, we feel that the times are hardening again, laden as they are with dark clouds. We experienced a brief moment during which social constraints and impositions were reduced: now they are reappearing in the foreground, albeit in new shapes. Now that genetic technologies, liberal globalization and human rights are triumphing, the label 'postmodern' is starting to look old; it has exhausted its capacities to express the world now coming into being.

The 'post' of postmodern still directed people's attentions to a past that was assumed to be dead; it suggested that something had disappeared without specifying what was becoming of us as a result, as if it were a question of preserving a newly conquered freedom in the wake of the dissolution of social, political and ideological frameworks.[1] Hence the success with which it met. That era is now ended. Hypercapitalism, hyperclass, hyperpower, hyperterrorism, hyperindividualism, hypermarket, hypertext – is there anything that isn't 'hyper'? Is there anything now that does not reveal a modernity raised to the nth power? The climate of epilogue is being followed by the awareness of a headlong rush forwards, of unbridled modernization comprised of galloping commercialization, economic deregulation, and technical and scientific developments being unleashed with effects that are heavy with threats as well as promises. It all happened very quickly: the owl of Minerva was announcing the birth of the postmodern just as the hypermodernization of the world was already coming into being.

Far from modernity having passed away, what we are seeing is its consummation, which takes the concrete form of a globalized liberalism, the quasi-general commercialization of lifestyles, the exploitation 'to death' of instrumental reason, and rampant individualism. Previously, the functioning of modernity was framed or shackled by a whole set of counterweights, alternative models and alternative values. The spirit of tradition continued to live on in different social groups; the division of roles between the sexes was still structurally unequal; the Church still held a tight grip on people's consciences; revolutionary parties were promising a different society, freed from capitalism and class conflict; the ideal of the Nation gave legitimacy to the supreme sacrifice of individuals; the State administered numerous activities in economic life. But now, everything has changed.

The society that is coming into being is one in which the forces opposing democratic, liberal and individualistic modernity are ineffectual, in which the great alternative visions have collapsed, in which modernization no longer meets with any strong organizational or ideological resistance. Not all pre-modern elements have evaporated, but they themselves function in accordance with a modern logic that is deregulated and de-institutionalized. Even social classes and class cultures are fading away before the principle of autonomous individuality. The State is on the retreat, religion and the family are being privatized, a market society is imposing itself: the cult of economic and democratic competition, technocratic ambition, and the rights of the individual all go unchallenged. A second modernity, deregulated and globalized, has shot into orbit: it has no opposite, and is absolutely modern, resting essentially on three axiomatic elements constitutive of modernity itself: the market, technocratic efficiency and the individual. We had a limited modernity: now is the time of consummate modernity.

In this context, the most diverse spheres are seeing a rising tide of extremism, in thrall to a boundless dynamic, a hyperbolic spiral.[2] Thus we are witnessing a formidable expansion in the size and number of financial and stock-market activities, an acceleration in the speed of economic operations that now function in real time, and a phenomenal explosion in the volume of capital circulating across the planet. For a long time, the consumer society paraded its own excess and the profusion of its merchandise: this has become even more so, thanks to hypermarkets and shopping centres that are increasingly gigantic and offer a whole plethora of all kinds of products, brands and services. In every domain there is a certain excessiveness, one that oversteps all limits, like an excrescence: witness different technologies and the mind-blowing ways in which they have overthrown the boundaries of death, food or procreation. The same thing can be seen in the images of the body produced in the hyperrealism of porn; television and the shows it broadcasts that play with the idea of total transparency; the Internet galaxy and its deluge of digital streams: millions of sites, billions of pages and characters, doubling in numbers every year; tourism and its cohorts of holiday-makers; urban agglomerations and their over-populated, asphyxiated, tentacular megalopolises. In the fight against terrorism and crime, millions of cameras and other electronic means of surveillance and citizen identification have already been installed in the streets, shopping centres, public transport and businesses: taking over from the old disciplinary and totalitarian society, the society of hypersurveillance is on the march. The frenzied escalation of 'more, always more' has now infiltrated every sphere of collective life.

Even individual behaviour is caught up in the machinery of excess: witness the mania for consumption, the practice of drug-taking in athletics, the vogue for extreme sports, the phenomenon of serial killers, bulimia and anorexia, obesity, compulsions and addictions. Two opposite trends can be discerned. On the one hand, more than ever, individuals are taking care of their bodies, are obsessed by health and hygiene, and obey medical guide-lines. On the other hand, individual pathologies are proliferating, together with the consumption characteristic of *anomie*, and anarchic behaviour. Hypercapitalism is accompanied by its double: a detached hyperindividualism, legislating for itself but sometimes prudent and calculating, sometimes unrestrained, unbalanced and chaotic. In the functional universe of technology, dysfunctional behaviour is on the increase. Hyperindividualism does not coincide merely with the interiorization of the model of *homo oeconomicus*, pursuing the maximization of his own interests in most spheres of life (education, sexuality, procreation, religion, politics, trades union activities), but also with the destructuring of the old social forms by which behaviour was regulated, with a rising tide of pathological problems, psychological disturbances and excessive behaviour. Through its operations of technocratic normalization and the loosening of social bonds, the hypermodern age simultaneously manufactures order and disorder, subjective independence and dependence, moderation and excess.

The first version of modernity was extreme in ideological and political terms; the new modernity is extreme in a way that goes beyond the political – extreme in terms of technologies, media, economics, town planning, consumption, and individual pathology. Pretty much everywhere, hyperbolic and sub-political processes now comprise the new face of liberal democracies. Not everything is dancing to the tune of excess, but nothing is safe, one way or another, from the logic of the extreme.

It is just as if we had moved from the 'post' era to the 'hyper' era. A new society of modernity is coming into being. It is no longer a matter of emerging from the world of tradition to reach the stage of modern rationality, but of modernizing modernity itself[3] and rationalizing rationalization: in other words, destroying 'archaic survivals' and bureaucratic

routines, putting an end to institutional rigidities and pro-
tectionist shackles, privatizing everything and freeing it
from dependency on local conditions, while sharpening competition. The heroic will to create a 'radiant future' has
been replaced by managerial activism: a vast enthusiasm for
change, reform and adaptation that is deprived of any confi-
dent horizon or grand historical vision. Everywhere the
emphasis has been placed on the need to keep moving, on
hyperchange unburdened of any utopian aims, dictated by
the demands of efficiency and the need to survive. In hypermodernity, there is no longer any choice or alternative other
than that of constantly developing, accelerating the movement so as not to be overtaken by 'evolution': the cult of
technocratic modernization has won out over the glorifica-
tion of ends and ideals. The less foreseeable the future, the
more we need to be mobile, flexible, ready to react, permanently prepared to change, supermodern, more modern than
the moderns of the heroic period. The mythology of a radical
break with the past has been replaced by the culture of the
fastest and the 'ever more': more profitability, more performance, more flexibility, more innovation.[4] It remains to be
seen whether this really means blind modernization, technocratic commodity nihilism, a process spinning round and
round in a vacuum without aim or meaning.

The modernity of the second sort[5] is the one which, at
peace with its basic principles (democracy, human rights,
the market) has no credible model to be set against it, and
never stops recycling within its own system the pre-modern
elements that were once objects to be eradicated. The
modernity from which we are emerging negated its other:
supermodernity integrates it. No longer the destruction of
the past but its reintegration, its reformulation in the framework of the modern logic of the market, of consumption
and individuality. When even the non-modern reveals the
primacy of the self and functions in accordance with a post-
traditional process, when the culture of the past no longer
poses any obstacle to individualistic and free-market modernization, a new phase of modernity appears. From 'post' to

'hyper': postmodernity will have been merely a transitional stage, a short-lived moment.[6] It is no longer ours.

These are all major upheavals which invite us to examine a little more closely the way social time is organized so as to govern the age in which we live. The past is resurfacing. Anxieties about the future are replacing the mystique of progress. The present is assuming an increasing importance as an effect of the development of financial markets, the electronic techniques of information, individualistic lifestyles and free time. Everywhere the speed of operations and exchanges is accelerating; time is short and becomes a problem looming at the heart of new social conflicts. The ability to choose your time, flexitime, leisure time, the time of youth, the time of the elderly and the very old: hypermodernity has multiplied divergent temporalities. To the deregulations of neo-capitalism there corresponds an immense deregulation and individualization of time. While the cult of the present makes its presence felt ever more sharply, what is the exact shape it is taking, and what are its links with the other temporal axes? How, on this axis, is the relation to future and past articulated? We need to reopen the dossier on social time: more than ever it requires investigation. To go beyond the way postmodernism envisaged these questions, and to reconceptualize the temporal organization that is being put into place: this is the object of the present study.

The Two Ages of the Present

Jean-François Lyotard was one of the first to note the link between the postmodern condition and 'presentist' temporality. The loss of credibility of progressivist systems, the pre-eminence of the norms of efficiency, the commercialization of knowledge, the increasing number of temporary contracts in everyday life:[6] what could all of this mean if not that the centre of temporal gravity of our societies has shifted from the future to the present? Defined by the way doctrines of emancipation had run out of steam, and by the rising influence of a type of legitimation centred on efficiency, the so-called postmodern period came in tandem with the predominance of the here-and-now.

Let us raise the question: what are the social and historical forces that have led to the death of the triumphalist visions of the future? Let us be clear: never could the failures or catastrophes of political and economic modernity (the two world wars, the totalitarian regimes, the Gulag, the Shoah, the crises of capitalism, the gap between North and South), by themselves, have entailed the ruin of the 'metanarratives', unless new reference points had succeeded, massively, in reshaping people's mentalities and offering new perspectives on their lives. Political disillusions and disappointments do not explain everything: there were, simultaneously, new passions, new dreams, new seductions exerting their influence day after day – not announced in bold letters, admittedly, but all-pervasive and affecting the vast majority of people. It was with the revolution in everyday life, with the profound upheavals in aspirations and lifestyles brought about by the last half-century, that the worship of the present came into being.

At the heart of the reordering of the way social time is organized lies the move from a capitalism of production to an economy of consumption, the replacement of an unbending and disciplinary society by a 'society of fashion' restructured from top to bottom by the technologies of ephemerality, novelty and permanent seduction. From industrially produced goods to leisure, from sports to games, from advertising to information, from hygiene to education, from beauty to diet: everywhere we are witnessing the spread of an accelerated obsolescence in the products and models on offer as well as multiform mechanisms of seduction: novelty, hyperchoice, do-it-yourself, not just well-being but better-being, humour, entertainment, solicitude, eroticism, travel, leisure. The world of consumption and mass communication appears like a waking dream, a world of seduction and ceaseless movement, whose model is none other than the system of fashion. No longer, as in traditional societies, do we see a repetition of the models of the past, but quite the opposite: systematic novelty and temptation act to regulate and organize the present. By spreading to broader and broader sectors of collective life, fashion, now ubiquitous, has established the axis of the present as the mode of temporality now socially prevalent.[7]

While the principle of fashion ('new, and better than ever before!') has imposed itself as without rivals, the cult of the new is asserting itself as an everyday and widespread passion. Societies reorganized by the logic and the very temporality of fashion have taken root: in other words, they are dominated by the present, which replaces collective action by private happiness, tradition by movement, hopes for the future by the ecstasy of permanent novelty. A whole hedonistic and psychologistic culture has come into being: it incites everyone to satisfy their needs immediately, it stimulates their clamour for pleasure, idolizes self-fulfilment, and sets the earthly paradise of well-being, comfort and leisure on a pedestal. Consume without delay, travel, enjoy yourself, renounce nothing: the politics of a radiant future have been replaced by consumption as the promise of a euphoric present.

In this way, the pre-eminence of the present has established itself less by moving in to occupy a lack (of meaning, value and any historical project) and more by promoting an excess of goods, images and hedonistic temptations. It is the power of the sub-political mechanisms of consumerism and ubiquitous fashion that has led to the routing of the ideological and political heroism of modernity. The consecration of the present began long before reasons for hoping in a better future collapsed: it started several decades earlier than the fall of the Berlin Wall or the accelerated universe of cyberspace and globalized liberalism.

The social consecration of the consumerist present has been accompanied by a plethora of accusations hurled against social atomization and depoliticization, the fabrication of false needs, consumerist conformism and passivity, and the gadgetization of an aimless and meaningless life. Moreover, from the 1970s onwards, the theme of the 'damage done by progress' started to find a significant echo. But none of these critiques have in any way prevented the rise of what can indeed be called a certain social optimism. Just when the last revolutionary incantations, heavy with hopes for the future, were still echoing, we saw the immediate present turned into an absolute, glorifying subjective authenticity and the spontaneity of desire in a culture of 'I want everything, now!' that made untrammelled pleasures a sacred right, without any worries about tomorrow. While May 1968 arose as a rebellion without any future aim, being both anti-authoritarian and libertarian, the years in which everyday morals became emancipated replaced commitment with enjoyment, and heroic history with 'desiring machines': it was exactly as if the present had succeeded in channelling all passions and dreams into itself. Unemployment rates were still tolerable, so worries about the future carried less weight than the desire to liberate the present and enjoy it as much as possible. The Thirty Glorious Years [of the post-1945 period in France], the Welfare State, the mythology of consumption, the counter-culture, the emancipation of morals and behaviour, the sexual revolution: all these phenomena succeeded in eradicating any sense of historical tragedy by establishing an awareness more optimistic than pessimistic, and a *Zeitgeist* that was dominated by an absence of anxiety about the future, thereby comprising a *carpe diem* at once anti-establishment and consumerist.

We have moved beyond this stage. From the 1980s and, especially, 1990s, onwards, a second-generation presentism has come into being, based on neo-liberal globalization and the revolution in information technologies. These two series of phenomena have combined to 'compress space-time' and boost the logic of acceleration. On the one hand, electronic and computerized media have made it possible to send and exchange information in 'real time', creating a sense of simultaneity and immediacy which increasingly makes all forms of waiting and slowness seem unacceptable. On the other hand, the increasing grip of the market and of financial capitalism has blocked any long-term visions of the State and replaced them with short-term performance, the accelerated circulation of capital on a global scale, and economic transactions that move in ever more rapid cycles.[8] Everywhere, the key-words that rule organizations are flexibility, profitability, 'beat the deadline', 'time is money', zero delay: and all of these trends bear witness to an exacerbated modernism that is gripping time ever more tightly in a logic of urgency. While neo-liberal, computerized society did not create the fever of the present, there can be no doubt that it brought it to its apogee by shuffling different time frames and intensifying our desire to be freed from the constraints of space-time.

One can go further: this reorganization of economic life has not been without dramatic consequences for entire categories of the population: 'capitalism in overdrive', and the priority given to immediate profitability, have led to massive reductions in staff numbers, to short-term employment, and to increased threats of unemployment. The spirit of the time dominated by frivolity has been replaced by a time of risk and uncertainty. A certain carefree attitude has gone for good: the present is increasingly lived out in a sense of insecurity.

The ambience of this civilization of ephemerality has changed the prevailing emotional tone. A sense of insecurity has invaded all minds; health has imposed itself as a mass obsession; terrorism, catastrophes and epidemics are regularly front-page news. Social struggles and critical discourses no longer carry any utopian perspectives that aim at overcoming domination. The only real question now is that of protection, security and the defence of social benefits, of urgent humanitarian aid and safeguarding the planet. In short, 'damage limitation'. The climate of the first period of presentism – liberating and optimistic – has faded, giving way to a now ubiquitous demand for protection.

The moment labelled 'postmodern' coincided with the trend to emancipate individuals from their social roles and traditional institutional authorities, as well as from the constraints inherent in group membership and pursuing distant aims and objectives; it is inseparable from the establishment of suppler and more diverse social norms, and from a broadening of the range of personal choices. As a result, we have seen a certain 'easing of tension', a sense of autonomy and openness in individual lives. Though it is synonymous with a certain disenchantment with the great collective projects, the postmodern parenthesis none the less became enveloped in a new form of re-enchantment, linked to the individualization of the conditions of life, the cult of the Self and private happiness. We have moved beyond this stage: the time of disenchantment with postmodernity itself has arrived – the time of the demythification of life lived in the present, now that it is forced to face the rising tide of insecurity. Instead of being lightened, our burden has become heavier; hedonism is on the retreat before our fears, the servitudes of the present seem more significant than the opening up of possibilities entailed by the individualization of society. On the one hand, the society of fashion endlessly incites us to enjoy the increasingly numerous pleasures of consumption, leisure and well-being. On the other, life is becoming less light-hearted, more stressful, more anxious. The increasing insecurity of people's lives has supplanted the carefree 'postmodern' attitude. Modernity of the second type appears as a paradoxical combination of frivolity and anxiety, euphoria and vulnerability, playfulness and dread. Within this context, the label 'postmodern' which announced a new birth has become, in its turn, a vestige of the past, a 'realm of memory'.

The Future's New Clothes

Has the axis of the present become a superpower in the temporal economy of our era? This can hardly be doubted: we live in a time of finance capitalism and precarious salaries, when a democracy of opinion reigns, together with the Internet and the 'throw-away' mentality. But how are we to conceptualize it? Is the prevailing temporal system equivalent, as some people suggest, to an 'absolute present', closed, wrapped up in itself, cut off from the past and the future? Does the contemporary individual really live in a state of 'temporal weightlessness', confined to a narrow immediacy emptied of every project and all heritage? Is he indistinguishable from 'the man of the present',[9] now a stranger to time, immersed in only one time – that of urgency and instantaneousness? Have the now ubiquitous acceleration, the feverish consumption, the effacement of traditions and utopias managed to create the civilization of the 'perpetual present', without past or future, of which Orwell spoke?[10] These ideas only partly tell the truth. The short-time economic flows, the bankruptcy of the progressivist ideas that used to be taken for granted, the collapse of the regulative power of traditions: all of these presentist phenomena are undeniable. However, in my view, they do not enable us to diagnose the outbreak of a culture of the 'eternal' or 'self-sufficient present'. Such a conceptualization ignores too much the paradoxical tensions which are active within the way that time is experienced in hypermodernity. The fact is that we have lost neither past nor future – the relationships to these dimensions have assumed a new and different importance in tandem with the way the present is extending its empire. There is no degree zero of temporality, of a 'self-referential' present consisting of radical indifference to what happened before and what will happen afterwards: the second kind of presentism that now rules our lives is no longer either postmodern or self-sufficient: it never ceases to open out on to something other than itself.

Confidence and the Future

There is no doubt that the period marked by the fears of technology and science, and the disintegration of political utopias, is also that of the 'crisis of the future'. There is no longer any faith in a future that will necessarily be better than the present, or any expectation of the final struggle and the Radiant City: the historical process used to be viewed as an absolute, but this has been followed by anxiety, the breakdown of any representations of the future, and the eclipse of the idea of progress. None the less, it is far from true that we have absolutely turned our backs on the idea of progress. While the mythology of continual and inevitable progress has become obsolete, we have nevertheless not ceased to expect and believe in the 'miracles of science': the idea of an improvement in the human condition by the applications of scientific knowledge is still meaningful. It is just that the relation to progress has become uncertain and ambivalent, since progress is associated not only with the promise of better things but also with the threat of a series of catastrophes. We are not witnessing the end of all belief in progress, but the emergence of a post-religious idea of progress, in other words an undefined and problematic future: a hypermodern future.

Modern societies came into being through a huge 'shift in time' that made the future more important than the present.[11] But this dominant temporality none the less brought back, in a secularized form, beliefs and mind-sets from the past, inherited from the spirit of religion (the unstoppable march towards happiness and peace, the utopia of the new man, the redemptive class, a society without divisions, the spirit of sacrifice). All these 'secular religions' laden with eschatological hopes have died out. In this sense, the 'lack of a future', or shrinking of the temporal horizon that is at the basis of hypermodern society, needs to be thought of as a secularization of modern representations of time, a process of disenchantment or modernization in the modern awareness of time itself. The decline in the mechanical cult of progress can no longer be confused with the 'absolute present' but rather with a *pure future*, one that needs to be constructed without any guarantees, without any pre-ordained path, or any implacable law of change.[12] A new stage in emancipation from the apron-strings of religion has been reached: this stage, the acme of modernity, is synonymous with the hypermodernization of our relationship to historical time.

The power of the future has not been destroyed: it is simply no longer ideological and political, but borne by the dynamic of technology and science. The more our period endorses the cult of democracy, now erected into a new absolute, the more laboratories start to imagine a dissimilar future and endeavour to produce a 'science fiction' universe, more incredible than fiction itself. The less one has a teleological vision of the future, the more that future lends itself to being manufactured in a hyperrealist way: science and technology in combination aspire to explore the infinitely great and the infinitely small, to reshape life, to manufacture mutants, to offer a semblance of immortality, to resurrect vanished species, to programme the genetic future. Never has humanity thrown down a greater challenge to man and space-time. Even if short-termism reigns in the economy and the media, our societies nevertheless continue to be turned to the future; they still wish to tear themselves away from the way things are – an impulse that is less romantic and, paradoxically, more revolutionary because it takes pains to make the impossible technically possible. Our inability to imagine the future increases, but it goes in tandem with a super-powerful science and technology more than able radically to transform the coming age: feverish short-termism is merely one of the faces of the future hypermodern civilization.

While the market extends its 'dictatorship' of short-termism, anxieties about the future of the planet and environmental risks are assuming a fundamental importance in the collective debate. Faced with the threats of atmospheric pollution, climate change, the erosion of biodiversity, and soil contamination, new ideas about 'sustainable development' and industrial ecology are being voiced: their basic concern is to transmit a viable environment to the generations that will succeed us. We are also seeing an increasing number of models simulating cataclysms, analyses of the risks faced at the national and planetary level, and estimates of the way things are likely to go, all aimed at discovering, evaluating and overcoming the dangers. Collective utopias are dying, and more pragmatic attitudes – involving foreseeing and forestalling the problems by technical and scientific means – are intensifying. While the axis of the present is still dominant, it is not absolute: the culture of prevention and the 'ethics of the future' have led to a renewed importance being given to the imperatives of a more or less distant future.

Doubtless, immediate economic interests come before attention to future generations. While we are witnessing the protests and chants of the virtuous, environmental destruction continues apace: there is a maximum number of appeals to everyone to be responsible, and a minimum number of actual public actions. The fact remains that worries about the future of the planet remain a live issue: they are a permanent feature of our awareness these days, keeping us on the alert, feeding into public controversies, calling for measures of protection for the natural heritage. The ever-present and all-absorbing claim of immediate profitability may be dominant, but it will not be so indefinitely. Even if eco-development is far from having at its disposal the technical means and regulatory systems it needs, it is starting, here and there, to stir people into action. Tomorrow, this dynamic should become more important. It is hardly likely that long-term awareness and constraints will have no effect; they will transform presentist practices as well as lifestyles and modes of development. The bases are being laid for a neo-futurism which will not resemble the old revolutionary futurism, imbued with the spirit of sacrifice: it is under the auspices of a reconciliation with the norms of the present (employment, economic profitability, consumption, well-being) that a new orientation to the future is being sought.

The economic dynamic itself is not exhausted in the pure present. This dynamic constantly implies a fundamental relation to the future in so far as it rests on a continued rise in consumption and investment, which need confidence. Progressivist optimism is no longer on the agenda, but this does not mean that all possible expectations of the future have evaporated. Anthony Giddens has brought out how modernity was linked to confidence in the abstract systems of 'experts':[13] we might add that it also requires the confidence of its protagonists in the future as a condition of the development of economic activity. This confidence on the part of consumers, investors and company bosses is, as everyone knows, volatile, and these days is regularly measured by polls. Hypermodernity has not replaced faith in progress by despair and nihilism, but by an unstable, fluctuating confidence that varies with events and circumstances. As the motor driving the dynamic of investments and consumption, optimism in the future has shrunk: but it is not dead. Like everything else, the sense of confidence has broken away from institutions and become deregulated; it now manifests itself only as a series of ups and downs.

The Retreat of 'Carpe Diem'

The point has already been made above: a new social and cultural climate has been established, each day moving a little further away from the relaxed, carefree attitudes of the postmodern years. Now that employment is more precarious and unemployment persists, feelings of vulnerability, of professional and material insecurity, are on the increase, together with the fear of the devaluation of one's qualifications, of being over-qualified for one's job and sliding down the social scale. The younger generation is afraid of not finding any place in the world of work; the older generation is afraid of losing its place for good. Hence the need to qualify quite considerably the diagnoses that talk of a neo-Dionysian culture based on attention to the present alone and its desires of enjoyment here and now. In reality, it is less a *carpe diem* which characterizes the spirit of the time than anxiety about a future fraught with risk and insecurity. In this context, living from day to day no longer means achieving a life of one's own, freed from collective strait-jackets, but is, rather, a constraint imposed by the destructuring of the labour market. The consumerist fever for immediate satisfactions, the aspirations toward a playful and hedonistic lifestyle, have of course by no means disappeared – they are being unleashed more than ever: but they are enveloped in a halo of fears and anxieties. The optimistic, carefree attitude that accompanied the Thirty Glorious Years and the cycle of bodily liberation now appear as memories from the past: hypermodernity is less a matter of focus on the present moment and more a question of that moment retreating into the background, now that the future has become uncertain and precarious.

These days, young people start to become anxious about their choice of studies and the jobs those studies might lead to at a very early age. The Damocles sword of unemployment is impelling students to opt for prolonged courses of study, and to engage in a race for qualifications that are considered as insurance for the future. Parents too have taken on board the threats linked to hypermodern deregulation. Rare are those who consider that education's central objective is the immediate satisfaction of the child's desire: it is training for the future that comes first;[14] hence the rise, in particular, of educational consumerism, private lessons, and non-basic activities outside school. Their aim is to prepare young people for adult life but also, at the other end, to find long-term financial solutions for their retirement. At the moment, the reform of pensions systems, and the lengthening of the time people need to pay contributions, figure among the major reforms of democratic governments, and bring hundreds of thousands of demonstrators out on to the streets. What makes anyone think that our culture has turned its back on the future? On the contrary: the future is at the heart of contemporary anxieties and debates; it is more and more something to be foreseen and reorganized. What is in decline is not the importance of the future, but the postmodern ethos of *hic et nunc*.

The new attitudes towards health illustrate in a striking way how the future is fighting back. In a period when medical normalization is invading more and more territories in the social arena, health is becoming a ubiquitous preoccupation for a growing number of individuals of every age.

As a result, hedonistic ideals have been supplanted by the ideology of health and longevity. In the name of these, individuals are to a massive degree renouncing immediate satisfactions, improving and reorienting their daily behaviour. Medicine is longer content with treating the sick; it intervenes long before any symptoms appear, informs us about the risks we run, encourages us to go for check-ups, take tests, and change our lifestyles. A chapter has been closed: the ethics of instant gratification has yielded to the cult of health, to the ideology of prevention, vigilance towards disease, and the medicalization of existence. To foresee, to forestall, to plan, to prevent: what has taken over our individualized lives is an awareness always building bridges to tomorrow and the day after tomorrow.

Ever-greater vigilance, ever more tests, ever more prevention: eating healthily, losing weight, watching your cholesterol levels, not smoking, taking physical exercise, the narcissistic obsession with health and longevity – all go in tandem with the priority of the future over the present. And this leads us to correct Tocqueville's remark frequently quoted: 'no sooner do they [democratic men] despair of living forever, than they are predisposed to act as if they were to exist but for a single day.'[15] In view of the importance assumed by the problems of health and age, we are forced to observe that we are far from such an ethos: hyperindividualism is less a cult of the present moment than a projection into the future, less festive than hygienic, less a matter of the intense enjoyment of life than of the prevention of problems: the relation to the present increasingly absorbs the future into itself. The vanishing of distant horizons has led less to an ethic of the absolute instant than to a pseudo-presentism undermined by the obsession with what is still to come. The carefree culture of *carpe diem* is on the retreat: under the pressure exerted by the norms of prevention and health, it is not so much the plenitude of the instant which predominates but rather a divided and anxious present, haunted by viruses and the ravages of time. Man has not experienced any 'detemporalization': the hypermodern individual is still an individual-for-the-future, a future based around 'me'.

Other phenomena reveal the limits of presentist culture. The cult of liberation is no longer in fashion, but we still see numerous ways in which value is attributed to everything enduring. Even if couples are more fragile and more precarious, our age, in spite of everything, is placing renewed value on fidelity, and demonstrating a desire for stable relationships in people's love lives. We hear more about the dissatisfactions and frustrations attendant on one-night stands than we hear hymns to transient love affairs. Why does love remain an ideal, a mass aspiration, unless one reason is the value ascribed to the durability with which it is associated? And how can we understand the desire to have a child, a desire which is anything but obsolete, without presupposing that people still have an emotional investment in long-term relationships? It is quite obvious that the pure instant is very far from having colonized private existence through and through: hypermodern society has led to our demand for durability gaining a new lease of life as a counterweight to the anxieties brought about by the reign of ephemerality.

Time in Conflict, and Chrono-reflexivity

As Marx demonstrated clearly, in his masterly analyses, the economy of time is at the basis of the way modern capitalism works. Capitalism endeavours to reduce working time to a maximum even when it poses working time as the source of wealth: it is a system which rests on a major temporal contradiction that excludes man from his own work. These contradictions, as everyone knows, have not stopped growing. Simultaneously, now that everything is centred on the organization of working time, we have shifted from a world marked by an increase in the different kinds of social time, by way of the development of heterogeneous temporalities (free time, consumption, leisure, holidays, health, education, variable working hours, retirement age) that are accompanied by unprecedented tensions.[16] Hence the accumulation of problems in the organization and management of social time, as well as the new demands for flexible hours – for reorganization and greater elasticity, to be achieved by personalized arrangements that encourage people to choose their own timetables. The modern obsession with time is no longer given concrete form merely in the sphere of work, submitted as it is to the criteria of productivity: it has extended into every aspect of life. Hypermodern society appears as the society in which time is increasingly experienced as a major preoccupation, one in which an increasing pressure on time is exerted in ever wider ways.

These temporal contradictions are echoed in everyday life and cannot be explained exclusively by the principle of economy and profitability transposed from production to the other spheres of social life. When we privilege the future, we have the feeling that we are missing out on 'real' life. Should we enjoy pleasures as they come, or else ensure that we will still have enough vitality for the years to come (health, figure, beauty)? Should we give time to our children or to our career? There is not just an acceleration in the rhythms of life, but also a subjective conflict that arises in our relation to time. Class antagonisms have lost their edge, while personal, temporal tensions are growing sharper and more general. It is no longer class against class, but time against time, future against present, present against future, present against present, present against past. What are we to choose as most important, and how can we fail to regret this or that option, when time has been torn away from tradition and made a matter for individual choice? The reduction in working hours, the growth of leisure, and the process of individualization have led to the escalation of themes and conflicts linked to time. The current trend is for singularized time-wars fought in the arena of subjective experience. The objective contradictions of productivist society are now accompanied by a spiral in existential contradictions.

The state of war against time implies that individuals are less and less trapped in the present alone: the dynamic of individualization and the means of information function as instruments of distancing, introspection and an inward-looking attitude.[17] Hypermodernity is not the same as a 'process without subject'; it is inseparable from self-expression, self-consciousness and consciousness-raising among individuals, paradoxically accentuated by the ephemeral action of the media. On the one hand, we are increasingly subjected to the constraints of rapid time, and on the other hand there is a growth in people's independence, and in their ability to make subjective choices and reflect on themselves. In individual-ized societies, freed from tradition, nothing can be taken for granted any more: the organization of existence and timetables demands arbitration and rectification, forecasts and information. We need to think of modernity as a meta-modernity, based on a chrono-reflexivity.

Accelerated Time and Time Regained

One of the most perceptible consequences of the power of the presentist agenda is the climate of pressure that it exerts on the lives of organizations and individual people. Several executives have pointed out what a frenzied rhythm domi-nates the mechanism of life in a company, now that global competition and the diktats of financial logic are the order of the day. There are ever more demands for short-term results, and an insistence on doing more in the shortest pos-sible time and acting without delay: the race for profits leads to the urgent being prioritized over the important, immedi-ate action over reflection, the accessory over the essential. It also leads to creating an atmosphere of dramatization, of per-manent stress – as well as a whole host of psychosomatic dis-orders. Hence the idea that hypermodernity is distinguished by the way the reign of urgency has become ubiquitous and turned into an ideological matter.[18]

The effects induced by the new order of time go far beyond the world of work: they find concrete expression in people's relation to everyday life, to themselves and others. Thus it is that an increasing number of people – women more than men, thanks to the constraints of the 'double day' – complain about being overwhelmed, of 'running to stand still', of being overworked. And now there is no age category that seems to be able to escape this headlong rush: pensioners and children too now have an overloaded timetable. The faster we go, the less time we have. Modernity was built around the critique of the exploitation of working time; hypermodern time registers a feeling that time is being increasingly rarefied. These days, we are more aware of the lack of time than we are of a widening in the number of possibilities entailed by the growth of individualization; we complain less about being short of money or freedom than about being short of time.

But while some people never have enough time, others (the unemployed, or young people in jail) have too *much* time. On the one hand we have the enterprising, hyperactive individual, enjoying the speed and intensity of time; on the other the individual with nothing better to do, crushed by the empty periods of his or her life.[19] It is hardly debatable that our ways of experiencing time are, as this suggests, twofold: what we are witnessing is the reinforcing of new forms of social inequality with regard to time. These new forms should not, however, conceal the global dynamic which, beyond specific groups or classes, has transformed from top to bottom the relationship of individuals to social time. By creating a hypermarket of lifestyles, the world of consumption, leisure, and (now) of new technologies has made possible a growing independence from collective temporal constraints: as a result, individual activities, rhythms and itineraries have become de-synchronized. The reign of the social present acts as a vector for the individualization of aspirations and behaviour, and it is accompanied by out-of-step rhythms and more personalized ways of constructing one's timetable.

Individualism has become polarized – as excess or lack – and can assert itself only against the background of this now ubiquitous pluralization and individualization in the way we manage time. In this sense, hypermodernity is inseparable from the breakdown in traditional and institutional frameworks and the growing individualization of our relation to time, an overall phenomenon which, transcending as it does differences of class or group, goes far beyond the world of the victors in the struggle. The new sense of enslavement to accelerated time occurs only in parallel with a greater ability on the part of individuals to organize their own lives.

This is a new relationship to time, one that is also illustrated by consumerist passions. There is no doubt that shopaholics have found, in many cases, a mere second-best, a way of consoling themselves for the miseries of existence, of filling in the emptiness of their present and future. The presentist compulsion to consume and the shrinkage in the temporal horizon of our societies go hand in hand. But is this compulsion merely derivative, a Pascalian diversion, a flight from a world deprived of any imaginable future – one that has become chaotic and uncertain? In fact, the escalation of consumerism is nourished both by existential distress and by the pleasure associated with change, by the desire to intensify and reintensify, without end, the course of daily life. Perhaps this is where the fundamental desire of the hypermodern consumer lies: to rejuvenate his or her experience of time, to revivify it by novelties that present themselves as so many fresh starts. We need to think of hyperconsumption as an emotional rejuvenating experience, one that can start all over again an indefinite number of times. This does not exactly mean that it is Orwell's 'perpetual present' that defines us, but rather a desire for perpetual self-renewal and the renewal of the present. The consumerist fury expresses a rejection of time that has become worn-out and repetitive, a struggle against that ageing of the feelings that ordinarily accompanies our days. It is less the repression of death and finitude than an anguish at the prospect of becoming mummified, repeating one's life and not really feeling alive. To the question 'what is modernity?', Kant replied: growing out of one's state as a minor, becoming adult. In hypermodernity it is just as if a new priority were arising: that of perpetually becoming 'young' again. Our neo-philiac instinct is first and foremost a way of warding off the ageing of our subjective experience: the de-institutionalized, volatile individual, in thrall to hyperconsumption, is the person who dreams of resembling a Phoenix of the emotions.

Sensualism and Performance

The culture of immediacy has been the object of number-less critiques that are not always free of a certain facile apoca-lyptic tone. In the world of bustling activity, speed – it is said – replaces the bond between human beings, efficiency replaces the quality of life, and feverishness replaces the enjoyment of intense but fleeting pleasures. No more lazy relaxation or contemplation: no longer can you voluptuously let yourself go. What counts is self-transcendence, a high-voltage life, the abstract pleasures of omnipotence that are procured by accelerating intensities. While real relations of proximity are giving way to virtual exchanges, what is being established is a culture of hyperactive performance without concrete or sensory reality – one which gradually destroys the aims of the hedonistic lifestyle.

Let us beware of taking the part for the whole. For the era of urgency is also the one in which we are seeing the spread and the democratization of technologies of increased well-being, the rise of quality markets, the eroticization of femi-nine sexuality, and the vogue for sports such as skiing. Music, travel, landscapes and DIY home improvement are all enjoy-ing an unprecedented vogue. They are all activities and tastes which reveal an era in which mass pleasures are being made more sensual and aesthetic. Two tendencies exist together. The one that accelerates speeds tends to the disincarnation of pleasures; the other, on the contrary, leads to the aestheti-cization of enjoyment, the bliss of the senses, the quest for the quality of the moment. On the one hand we have a compressed time, one which is 'efficient' and abstract; on the other hand, a time centred on the qualitative, on bodily pleasures – one which aims to make the passing moment more sensual. It is in this way that ultra-modern society presents itself as a disunited and paradoxical culture. This is a yoking of contraries that merely intensifies two major principles constitutive of technocratic and democratic modernity: the conquest of efficiency and the ideal of earthly happiness.

Hedonist culture has been systematically analysed and stigmatized as an injunction to consumerist and erotic happiness, to the 'tyranny of pleasure' and the 'totalitarianism' of the market. But what do we see in reality? Cathedrals of consumption are flourishing, while spiritualities and ancient schools of wisdom are also in fashion; porn is flagrant and ubiquitous, while sexual habits are sensible rather than unbridled; cyberspace is making communication virtual, while individuals are voting overwhelmingly for live performances, collective parties, and evenings out with friends; paying for services is becoming the norm, while voluntary workers are becoming more numerous, and affection and emotion more than ever form the basis for the life of couples. It is obvious that the individual is no longer the faithful reflection of the hyperbolic logic of the media and the market; he is no more the 'slave' of the performance-obsessed sexual agenda than he is the mechanical product of advertising. Other motivations and other ideals (relational, intimate, amorous, ethical) continue ceaselessly to act as guide-lines for the hyperindividual. The reign of the present is less that of the normalization of happiness than that of the diversification of models, the erosion of the organizing power of collective norms, and the de-standardization of pleasures. The grip of the norms of consumption and sexuality grows all the stronger in that these factors provide less precise direction for individual behaviour.

The hypermodern individual may be over-active, but he is also prudent, concerned with affections and emotions and with relationships: the acceleration of speeds has abolished neither sensitivity to the other, nor the passion for qualitative experience, nor the aspiration to a 'balanced' life that finds place for the emotions. Extremism is merely one of the tendencies of ultra-modernity. Certain executives may be workaholics, but the majority of salaried employees aspire to a harmony between professional life and private life, work and leisure. Porn films can be freely hired, but people's libidinal lives are very far from having collapsed into an orgy of ubiquitous partner-swapping. Advertising may glorify the joys of the market, but it is one's relationships to other people (children, love, friendship) that comprise the quality of life for the vast majority. The frenzy of 'always more' does not kill off the qualitative logic of 'not more, but better' and the importance of feelings: it gives them, on the contrary, a greater social visibility, a new mass legitimacy. Everywhere, hypermodern hype is reined in by people's demands for a better quality of life, the value they place on feelings and on the irreplaceability of the individual; everywhere the logic of excess is reined in. Ultra-modern society, so affected by conflicting norms, is not one-dimensional; it resembles a paradoxical chaos, an organizing disorder.[20]

In this context, what ought to be worrying us the most is not the way pleasure has become desensualized or turned into a 'dictatorship', but the way in which people's personalities have become more fragile. Hypermodern culture is characterized by the weakening of the regulative power of collective institutions and the corresponding way in which actors have become more autonomous *vis-à-vis* group imperatives, whether these come from family, religion, political parties or class cultures. Hence the individual appears more and more opened up and mobile, fluid and socially independent. But this volatility signifies much more a destabilization of the self than a triumphant affirmation of a subject endowed with self-mastery – witness the rising tide of psychosomatic symptoms and obsessive-compulsive behaviour, depression, anxiety and suicide attempts, not to mention the growing sense of inadequacy and self-deprecia- tion. This psychological vulnerability is less the result, as is too often claimed, of the extenuating weight of performance norms, or the intensification of the pressures exerted on people, and more a matter of the breakdown of the previous systems of defence and other frameworks that supported the individual. Let us just remember that this flaring up of anxiety and depression *preceded* the triumph of entrepreneurial culture and neo-liberalism. It is not so much the pressures of the performance culture that explain the phenomenon: rather, we need to look to the formidable growth in individualization, the decline in the organizational power of the collective over its subjects. Abandoned to himself, deprived of any framework, the individual finds himself deprived of the social structures that endowed him with an inner strength that enabled him to face up to life's trials and tribulations. Widespread institutional deregulation is accompanied by mood swings, an increasing lack of organization in people's personalities, a growth in the number of psychological disturbances and cries for help. It is the extreme individualization of our societies that, after weakening people's 'inner' resistances, underlies the spiral of subjective problems and unbalanced behaviour. Thus it is that the ultra-modern period is seeing the growth of technological power over space-time, but a simultaneous decline in the individual's inner strength. The less collective norms can command our behaviour in detail, the more the individual shows a growing tendency to be weak and unstable. The more socially mobile the individual is, the more we witness signs of exhaustion and subjective 'breakdowns'; the more freely and intensely people wish to live, the more we hear them saying how difficult life can be.

The Past Revisited

The 'return' of the future is not the only phenomenon which undermines the idea that the social present has eyes only for itself: the revival of the past that we are witnessing also suggests that we ought to rectify such an idea.

It is undeniable that, in celebrating the pleasures of the here-and-now and the latest thing, consumerist society is continually endeavouring to make collective memory wither away, to accelerate the loss of continuity and the abolition of any repetition of the ancestral. The fact remains that, far from being locked up in a self-enclosed present, our age is the scene of a frenzy of commemorative activities based on our heritage and a growth in national and regional, ethnic and religious identities. The more our societies are dedicated followers of fashion, focused on the present, the more they are accompanied by a groundswell of memory. The moderns wanted to make a *tabula rasa* of the past, but we are rehabilitating it; their ideal was to break away from the grip of traditions, but those traditions have acquired a new social dignity. Celebrating the slightest object from the past, invoking the duties of memory, remobilizing religious traditions, hypermodernity is not structured by an absolute present, it is structured by a *paradoxical present*, a present that ceaselessly exhumes and 'rediscovers' the past.

Memory in the Age of Hyperconsumption

It is sometimes said, jokingly, that one new museum opens every day in Europe, and that we have lost count of the celebrations of anniversaries of the great (and less great) events of history. These days, is there any object that cannot be museified, restored, celebrated? Absolutely any date, from the tenth to the fiftieth, and from the twentieth to the one-hundred-and-fiftieth anniversary, is the pretext for some festivity. Soon there will be no activity left, no object, no locality, that does not have the honours of a museum or museum-type institution. From the museum of pancakes to the museum of the sardine, from the Elvis Presley museum to the museum of the Beatles, hypermodern society belongs to an age where everything is made into part of our heritage and duly commemorated.

In this emphasis on the value of the past, we can of course recognize a typically 'postmodern' symptom. However, the end of modernism – which negated anything old – does not spell the eclipse of the modern. On the contrary, a number of characteristics of the phenomenon point to a new wave of cultural modernization. The formidable expansion in the number of objects and signs that are deemed worthy to belong to the memory of our heritage, the proliferation of museums of every kind, the obsession with commemorations, the mass democratization of cultural tourism, the threat of degradation or paralysis hanging over heritage sites because of the overwhelming floods of tourists – this whole new insistence on everything old is accompanied by an unbridled expansion, a saturation, a boundless broadening of the frontiers of our heritage and our memory: and in these we can recognize a modernization taken to its logical conclusion. We have moved from the realm of the finite to that of the infinite, from the limited to the ubiquitous, from memory to the hypermemorial: in neo-modernity, the excess of presentist logic goes together with a proliferating inflation of memory.

This ultra-modernity is also revealed by the emphasis placed, to an increasing extent, on the economic impact of the preservation of our heritage, on criteria of direct or indirect profitability in a sphere that used to be imbued by the cult of the nation and the spirit of public service. The naming of streets and the erection of statues have now been supplanted by commemorations that are exploited by the publishing and media industries, unleashing onto the market dozens of titles of books, re-editions, cartoon strips, films and television films. The monument used to be a symbol, and its preservation was an end in itself: now the financial costs of maintaining it are justified by its financial fall-out, by tourist development or the media image of towns and regions. These are geological 'deposits' to be exploited and promoted: the old buildings have been hijacked, revamped, converted into cultural centres, museums, hotels, theatres or offices; the historic town centres are given a spring-clean and spruced up, transformed into products for cultural and tourist consumption. And everywhere we see the setting up of car parks, cafeterias, souvenir shops, and performances of folklore.[21] In ultra-modern society, the model of the market and its operational criteria have succeeded in infiltrating even the way we safeguard our heritage. The value attributed to the past is a symptom of the advance of cultural capitalism and the commercialization of culture: as such, it is less a postmodern than a hypermodern phenomenon.

When the heritage industry triumphs, the citizen gives way to consumer man. The old solemn and 'sedentary' style characteristic of commemorations, a style which aimed at permanently inscribing memory on to the very sites of the past, is in retreat before a 'frivolous' and ephemeral style limited basically to the moment of celebration and to that alone: colloquia, concerts, exhibitions, happenings, performances, creative parades.[22] Museums put on historical shows, and archaeological sites create virtual simulations to bring the past to life; the 'tourism of memory' is experiencing a mass success. The works of the past are no longer contemplated in meditative silence, but 'gobbled up' in a few seconds, functioning as a way of entertaining the masses, an attractive spectacle, a method for diversifying leisure and 'killing' time. The new lease of popularity being enjoyed by the past illustrates the advent of the world of consumption and the coming of the hyperconsumer who is less in search of something that will make him feel 'distinguished' than of perpetual stimulation, emotions-per-second, recreational activities. It is not modernity that is being buried, but the third stage of consumerist modernity that is triumphing[23] in the mass democratization of cultural leisure, the consumerism of experience, the transformation of memory into entertainment and spectacle.

The vogue for the past can also be seen in the success of old objects, of antique hunting, of everything that mimics the past, everything 'vintage', all the products stamped 'authentic' that arouse our nostalgia. More and more, businesses are referring to their history, making the most of their heritage, communicating with their past, launching products that encapsulate memories and make the old times come alive again. Shop signs present articles from our heritage, and several brand names suggest 'old-style recipes' and products inspired by ancestral traditions. In hypermodern society, everything old, and our nostalgia for it, have become sales techniques and marketing tools.

This come-back of the past comprises one of the facets of the cosmos of the hyperconsumption of experience: it is no longer just a matter of gaining access to material comfort, but of buying and selling reminiscences, emotions that evoke the past, and memories of days deemed to have been more glamorous. There was use-value and exchange-value: in addition, we now have the emotional-memorial value associated with feelings of nostalgia. This is a phenomenon that is indissociably postmodern and hypermodern. 'Post' because it is turned towards the past. 'Hyper' because what we now see is the marketing and consumption of our relationship to time, and the expansion of commercial logic into the territory of memory.

While an interest in the past is thus finding expression, daily life, for its part (hygiene, health, leisure, consumption, education), is regulated, more than ever, by the mobile order of the present. Food products are labelled 'authentic', but they are commercialized in accordance with the techniques of mass marketing, adapted to contemporary tastes, and manufactured in conformity with the current norms of hygiene and security. The old blocks of flats in town centres are being rehabilitated, but now they have all mod cons. Our awareness of the value of our heritage is becoming more intense, but what we produce has a shorter and shorter shelf-life. The past no longer provides a social foundation or structure: it is revamped, recycled, updated, exploited for commercial ends. Tradition no longer calls for the faithful repetition and revival of the way things were always done: it has become a nostalgic product to be consumed, a piece of folklore, a wink and a nod at the past, an *object of fashion*. In its institutional guise it used to regulate the collective whole: its value now is merely aesthetic, emotional and playful. There may be a frenzied vogue for the past, but it no longer has the power to organize collectively the way people behave. The past seduces us, while the present and its changing norms govern us. The more we summon up historical memory and dramatize it, the less it structures the elements of ordinary life. Hence this characteristic of hypermodern society: we celebrate what we no longer wish to take as an example.[24]

In centuries ruled by custom, according to Tarde, the past functions as a prestigious model to be imitated. This is no longer true in our own time, where it appears increasingly to be a background, an index of quality or security of life. For everything 'authentic' has a reassuring effect on our sensibilities: associated with an imaginary scene of closeness, conviviality, the 'good old days' (the village, the craftsman, the love of one's work), 'old-style' products banish the anxieties of neo-consumers obsessed with security and mistrustful of the way in which food has become industrialized. Likewise, the heritage effect is also part of the same culture of individualist well-being. Dormitory towns, tower blocks and railings, the tarmacking over of the seashore – all of this has led to the desire to safeguard old landscapes and the buildings of the past, all seen as forms of resistance to ugliness, to an encroaching functional and technological uniformity. If doting on the past has a nostalgic dimension, it also bears witness to the rising power of individualistic desires for quality of life, and to a hypermodern culture of well-being inseparable from criteria that are more qualitative and sensorial, more aesthetic and cultural. Together with a taste for the past, we increasingly see hyper-individualistic passions for 'comfort and pleasure' and 'existential comfort',[25] the new demand for agreeable sensations, for a high-quality ambience and environment.

It is probable that the obsession with memory will not be perpetuated indefinitely: certain signs already indicate, perhaps, a certain ebbing.[26] A day will come when the proliferation of heritage sites and commemorations will reach its limit and no longer rouse such enthusiasm. However, we can bet that there will not be a return to the modernist cult of the blank page. The second age of modernity is self-reflexive, individualist-emotional and concerned with identity: it is revolutionary in the technical and scientific domain, but no longer so in culture. It is not the same as the depreciation of the past, but comprises rather the unhampered exploitation and mobilization of every axis of social and historical temporality, the recycling and reshaping of memory to economic and emotional ends, always with an eye to one's identity. Even if the tidal wave of memory overwhelming us finally subsides, it will not just vanish. Commerce, fashion and the demand for greater well-being, as well as desires stemming from one's sense of identity, should for a long time to come treat memory as a resource and a necessity for the presentist order of things.

Identity and Spirituality

The way the past has come back into favour goes way beyond the mimicry of antiques and the cult of heritage and its commemorations. It finds concrete form, with even greater intensity, in the awakening of spiritualities and the new quest for identity. Religious renewal, national and regional demands, the ethnic revival: in all these guises, contemporary societies are witnessing a rise in the importance of guide-lines that point back to the past, a need for continuity between past and present, a longing to find one's roots and discover one's history. Technological and commercial globalization may be bringing about a homogenized temporality, but the fact remains that this occurs in tandem with a process of cultural and religious fragmentation that mobilizes myths and foundation stories, symbolic inheritances, and historical and traditional values.

It is well known how, in several cases, the reactivation of historical memory functions in frontal opposition to the principles of liberal modernity – witness the upsurge in religious trends which reject secular modernity, the neo-nationalist and ethnic and religious movements that lead to dictator-ships, wars of identity, and genocidal massacres. The end of the division of the world into blocs, the ideological vacuum, the globalization of the economy, and the weakening of state power have led to the rise of a multitude of local conflicts based on ethnic, religious or national factors, together with separatist movements and wars between communities. Neo-nationalist and ethnic and religious upsurges, rejecting the pluralism of open societies, cleansing society of all 'hetero-geneous' elements, and closing communities in on them-selves, are in one place accompanied by the struggle against Westernization, in another by devastating wars, repression and politico-religious terrorism. Is this the reawakening of old demons? But it would be wrong to interpret these phe-nomena as resurgences or repetitions of the past, whether that past be tribal or totalitarian. Even if people are falling back on an identity politics that means reviving older men-talities, it is unprecedented forms of conflict, nationalism and democracy that are starting to appear. Behind appeals to the preservation of national or religious identity, tyrannies of a new kind are being set up, together with combinations of democracy and ethnicity, frustrated modernization and all-conquering 'fundamentalism' – combinations which Fareed Zakaria quite rightly calls 'illiberal democracies'.[27]

This being so, all movements that rekindle the flame of the sacred or seek for roots are very far from being similar, or from having the same links with liberal modernity. On the contrary, many of them in the West present themselves as having characteristics that are perfectly in accord with a liberal culture in which the individual legislates for his or her own life. Proof of this is provided by those *à la carte* reli-gions, those groups and networks that combine the spiritual traditions of East and West, and use the religious tradition as a means for their adepts to find self-fulfilment. Here there is no antinomy with individualist modernity, since the tradition is handed over to the initiative of individuals, 'cobbled together' in a DIY manner, mobilized for self-realization and integration into a community. The hypermodern age does not put an end to the need to appeal to traditions of sacred meaning: it merely revamps them to give them greater individuality, a wider spread, and a more intensely emotional set of beliefs and practices. With the pre-eminence granted to the axis of the present, we see a rise in the number of deregulated religions and post-traditional identities.

Instrumental rationality is extending its domain, but this eliminates neither religious belief nor the need to refer to the authority of a tradition. On the one side, the process of rationalization forces the grip of religion on social life to weaken more and more; on the other, it re-creates, of its own momentum, demands for religiosity and a need for roots in a 'line of descent of believers'. Here, too, we should beware of seeing new spiritualities as a residual phenomenon, a regression or a pre-modern archaism. In fact, it is from *within* the hypermodern cosmos that the religious domain is reproduced, in so far as the hypermodern generates insecurity, the loss of fixed guide-lines, the disappearance of secular utopias, and an individualist disintegration of the social bond. In the uncertain, chaotic, atomized universe of modernity, new needs for unity and meaning, for security and a sense of belonging, arise: this is a new opportunity for religions. In any case, the march of secularization does not lead to an entirely rationalized world in which the social influence of religion is in a state of continual decline. Secularization is not irreligion; it is also a process which creates a new form of the religious domain in the sphere of worldly autonomy, a religious domain that is de-institutionalized, subjective and focused on the emotions.[28]

This remobilization of memory is inseparable from a new kind of collective identification. In societies ruled by tradition, religious and cultural identity was experienced as something self-evident, received and intangible, excluding individual choices. This is no longer the case. In the present situation, one's sense of identity and belonging is anything but instantaneous, given once and for all: it is a problem, a claim, an object for individuals to appropriate for themselves. Belonging to a community is a means of constructing oneself and saying who one is, a way of affirming oneself and gaining recognition: it is thus, inseparably, a means of self-definition and self-questioning. We are no longer Jewish, Muslim or Basque 'as easily as breathing'; we question our identities, we examine them, we want to appropriate for ourselves something which had hitherto gone without saying.[29] Cultural identity used to be institutional: now it has become open and reflexive, an individual gamble in which the dice can be thrown again and again.

The upsurge of particularist demands means that we need to correct the simplistic readings that reduce hyper-individualism to a frenzy of consumerist and competitive passions. While hyper-individualism cannot be separated from the consecration of private pleasures and individual merit, we are obliged to note that it is equally inseparable from a great increase in demands for public recognition, and also in demands for different cultures to be equally respected. It is no longer enough to be recognized by what we do, or as free citizens equal to everyone else: it is a question of being recognized by what we are in our specificity as part of a community and a history, by that which distinguishes us from other groups. This is the proof, among other things, that modernity of the second kind is not exhausted by the solipsistic torrent of consumerist appetites: in fact, it bears within itself a broadening of the ideal of equal respect, a desire for *hyper-recognition* which, rejecting every form of the contempt, depreciation or sense of inferiority under which one might suffer, demands the recognition of the other as equal in his or her difference. The reign of the hyper-modern present is, to be sure, that of the immediate satisfaction of needs, but it is also that of a moral demand for recognition broadened to identities based on gender, sexual orientation or historical memory.

This process of hyper-recognition is not unlinked to a mass society of individualist well-being. It is this society which, in Western democracies, has contributed to a decline in the value placed on the abstract principles of citizenship in favour of poles of identity that are more immediate and particularist in character. In a hyper-individualist society, we invest our emotions in what is closest to us, in links based on resemblance and common origin, since universalist values and great political ideals appear as principles that are too abstract, too general or remote.[30] By destroying revolutionary hopes, and focusing life on private happiness, the civilization of the present moment has paradoxically unleashed a desire for the recognition of the specific identity conferred by collective roots.

It is also the culture of individualist well-being that, by giving a new importance to the need for self-esteem and esteem for others, has made it impossible to accept suffering engendered by collective negative images imposed by dominant groups. In the era of happiness, everything which inculcates a negative image of oneself, or withholds recognition, is deemed illegitimate, and appears as a symbolic form of oppression or violence incompatible with the ideal of full self-realization. Hence the multiplication of demands for reparation in the case of collective offences, the expectation that everyone will be granted public recognition, and the ever-more-frequent clamourings for victim status. While demands for particularist recognition are inseparable from the modern democratic ideal of human dignity, it is, none the less, our presentist civilization which has made 'the politics of recognition' possible,[31] a politics that acts as an instrument of self-esteem, inculcates new responsibilities *vis-à-vis* the past, and fuels the new controversial debates over memory.

The contemporary galaxy of identities is also an opportunity for taking another look at the rich analyses of high modernity put forward by Ulrich Beck. According to this German sociologist, we have moved from a first stage of modernization based on the opposition between tradition and modernity to a second modernization, self-reflexive and self-critical in nature. In this latest phase, it is modernization itself which is considered as a problem attacking the spread of a scientistic mentality as well as the working bases of industrial society. Hence the idea of a new modernity, self-referential in type.[32]

This description is correct, but we need to take it further and make it more general. What we really need to point out is that the second cycle of modernity is not merely self-referential: it is marked by the return of traditional landmarks and of ethnic and religious demands based on types of symbolic heritage that go back a very long way and stem from diverse origins. In other words, all the memories, all the universes of meaning, all the forms of the collective imaginary that refer to the past and that can be drawn on and redeployed to construct identities and enable individuals to find self-fulfilment. Ultra-modern self-consciousness does not merely affect technological risks, scientific rationality or the division of sexual roles, it imbues all the repositories of meaning, all the traditions of East and West, all the different kinds of knowledge and belief, including the most irrational and the least orthodox: astrology, reincarnation, marginal sciences, etc. What defines hypermodernity is not exclusively the self-critique of modern institutions and forms of knowledge, but also revisionary memory, the remobilization of traditional beliefs, and the individualist hybridization of past and modernity. It is no longer a question merely of the deconstruction of traditions, but of the way they are used without any institutional backing, being perpetually reworked in accordance with the principle of individual sovereignty. If hypermodernity is meta-modernity, it also manifests itself in the guise of a meta-traditionality and a meta-religiosity without bounds.

There is no lack of phenomena which might justify a relativistic or nihilistic interpretation of the hypermodern universe. The dissolution of the unquestioned bases of knowledge, the primacy of pragmatism and the reign of money, the sense of the equal worth of all opinions and all cultures – these are all elements which feed into the idea that scepticism and the disappearance of higher ideals constitute a major characteristic of our epoch. Does observable reality in fact suggest that such a paradigm is correct?

While it is undeniable that many cultural landmarks have been displaced, and that a technocratic and commercial dynamic now organizes whole sectors of our societies, the fact remains that the collapse of meaning has not been taken to its logical conclusion, since that meaning continues to deploy itself against the background of a strong and broad consensus about the ethical and political foundations of liberal modernity. Beyond the 'war of the gods' and the growing power of the market, a hard core of shared values continues to assert itself, one which fixes strict limits to the steamroller advance of operational rationality. Our entire ethical and political heritage has not been eradicated: there are still checks and balances that prevent us from accepting the radical interpretation of hypermodern nihilism – in particular, ethical protests and commitments. The new consecration of human rights puts these right at the ideological centre of gravity as an omnipresent organizational norm of collective actions. It is not true that money and efficiency have become the motive force and ultimate aim of all social relations. How, if this were true, could we understand the value accorded to love and friendship? How could we explain the indignant reactions to new forms of slavery and barbarity? What gives rise to new demands for an ethical attitude in economic activity, the media and political life? Even if our epoch is the stage on which are played out the conflicts between a whole variety of different conceptions of the good, it is marked, at the same time, by an unprecedented reconciliation with its basic humanist foundations: never have these enjoyed such an unquestioned legitimacy. Not all values, not all benchmarks of meaning, have been blown apart: hypermodernity is not a question of 'ever greater instrumental performance, and therefore ever fewer values that have the force of obligations', but a technocratic and market-driven spiral that is accompanied by a unanimous endorsement of the common roots of humanist and democratic values.

No one will argue with the fact that the way the world is going arouses more anxiety than unbridled optimism: the gulf between North and South is widening, social inequalities are increasing, all minds are obsessed by insecurity, and the globalized market is reducing the power of democracies to govern themselves. But does this enable us to diagnose a process of world-wide 'rebarbarization' in which democracy is no longer anything more than a 'pseudo-democracy' and a 'decorative spectacle'?[33] This would be to underestimate the powers of self-critique and self-correction that continue to dwell in the liberal democratic universe. The presentist age is anything but closed, wrapped up in itself, doomed to an exponential nihilism. Because the depreciation of supreme values is not limitless, the future remains open. Democratic and market-led hypermodernity has not uttered its final word: it is merely at the start of its historic adventure.

NOTES

1 Krzysztof Pomian, 'Post-ou comment l'appeler?', *Le débat*, 60 (1990).
2 On excess as a figure of ultra-modernity, see Marc Augé, *Non-Places: Introduction to an Anthropology of Supermodernity*, tr. John Howe (London: Verso, 1995); Jean Baudrillard, *Fatal strategies*, tr. Philip Beitchman and W. G. J. Niesluchowksi, ed. Jim Fleming (New York: Semiotext(e); London: Pluto, 1990); Paul Virilio, *Vitesse et politique* (Paris: Galilée, 1977).
3 Ulrich Beck, *Risk Society: Towards a New Modernity*, tr. Mark Ritter (London: Sage, 1992).
4 Pierre-André Taguieff, *Résister au bougisme* (Paris: Mille et une nuits, 2001), pp. 75–85. See also Jean-Pierre Le Goff, *La Barbarie douce* (Paris: La Découverte, 1999).
5 The cycle that I have called the 'second individualist revolution' is analysed in *L'Ère du vide* (Paris: Gallimard, 1983).
6 Jean-François Lyotard, *The Postmodern Condition: A Report on Knowledge*, tr. Geoff Bennington and Brian Massumi (Manchester: Manchester University Press, 1984).
7 Gilles Lipovetsky, *The Empire of Fashion: Dressing Modern Democracy*, tr. Catherine Porter (Princeton: Princeton University Press, 1994), part II.
8 Manuel Castells, *The Rise of the Network Society*, 2nd edn (Oxford: Blackwell, 2000).

9 Zaki Laïdi, *Le Sacre du présent* (Paris: Flammarion, 2000). See also Pierre-André Taguieff, *L'Effacement de l'avenir* (Paris: Galilée, 2000), pp. 96–101.
10 Quoted in Jean Chesneaux, *Habiter le temps* (Paris: Bayard, 1996), p. 71.
11 See Krzysztof Pomian, 'La crise de l'avenir', *Le débat*, 7 (Dec. 1980).
12 Marcel Gauchet, *The Disenchantment of the World: A Political History of Religion*, tr. Oscar Burge (Princeton: Princeton University Press, 1997), pp. 183–5.
13 Anthony Giddens, *The Consequences of Modernity* (Cambridge: Polity, 1991), pp. 79–92.
14 On school as futurist institution, see Marcel Gauchet, 'L'école à l'école d'elle-même', in his book *La démocratie contre elle-même* (Paris: Gallimard, 2002), pp. 154–68.
15 Alexis de Tocqueville, *Democracy in America*, tr. by Francis Bowen (revised) (London: Everyman's Library, 1994), vol. II, book 2, ch. 17, pp. 149–50.
16 Roger Sue, *Temps et ordre social* (Paris: PUF, 1994).
17 I am radically opposed to the arguments that see in our temporal regime nothing more than 'impoverishing traps', 'a whirlwind flight', 'the mutilation of duration' that make any distance and any mediation impossible, as well as any 'reversibility of thought'; cf. Chesneaux, *Habiter le temps*.
18 Nicole Aubert, *Le Culte de l'urgence* (Paris: Flammarion, 2003).
19 Robert Castel, *Les Métamorphoses de la question sociale* (Paris: Fayard, 1995), pp. 461–74.
20 On this point, see my book *Le Crépuscule du devoir* (Paris: Gallimard, 1992).
21 On these points, see Françoise Choay, *L'Allégorie du patrimoine* (Paris: Seuil: 1992), pp. 163–76. See also Jean-Michel Leniand, *L'Utopie française: essai sur le patrimoine* (Paris: Merges, 1992).
22 Pierre Nora, 'The era of commemoration', in *Realms of Memory: Rethinking the French Past*, general ed. Pierre Nora, English-language edn ed. Lawrence D. Kritzman, tr. Arthur Goldhammer, iii: *Symbols* (New York: Columbia University Press, 1998), pp. 609–37. See also Thierry Gasnier, 'La France commémorante', *Le débat*, 78 (1994), pp. 95–8.
23 See my study, 'La société d'hyperconsommation', *Le débat*, 124 (2003).

24 William M. Johnston, *Postmodernisme et bimillénaire* (Paris: PUF, 1992), p. 16.

25 Claudette Sèze, 'La modification', in *Confort moderne: une nouvelle culture du bien-être, Autrement*, 10 (Jan. 1994), pp. 119–23.

26 Robert Hewison, 'Retour à l'héritage ou la gestion du passé à l'anglaise', *Le débat*, 78 (1994), p. 137. See also Pierre Nora, 'Era of commemoration', p. 637.

27 Fareed Zakaria, *From Wealth to Power: The Unusual Origins of America's World Role* (Princeton: Princeton University Press, 1998).

28 I am here drawing on the fine studies by Danièle Hervieu-Léger, *Religion as a Chain of Memory*, tr. Simon Lee (New Brunswick, NJ: Rutgers University Press, 2000), and *Le Pèlerin et le converti* (Paris: Flammarion, 1999).

29 Dominique Schnapper, *La France de l'intégration* (Paris: Gallimard, 1991), pp. 307–10.

30 Bela Farago, 'La démocratie et le problème des minorités nationales', *Le débat*, 76 (1993), pp. 16–17.

31 Charles Taylor, *Multiculturalism and 'The Politics of Recognition': An Essay*, with a commentary by Amy Gutman (Princeton: Princeton University Press, 1992).

32 Beck, *Risk Society*.

33 Taguieff, *Résister au bougisme*, p. 123.

STAGES IN AN INTELLECTUAL ITINERARY
A Conversation between Gilles Lipovetsky and Sébastien Charles

SC: *You are considered as something of a free electron in the French intellectual scene, and that fact needs explaining. One has the impression that polemics don't interest you, and that confrontation doesn't help you to develop your own works. How do you explain that?*

GL: A free electron? I don't know . . . But this impression is probably linked to the fact that I'm a philosopher who has 'strayed' into the analysis of social and historical realities and that, faced with these, my questioning is still, in spite of everything, marked by the philosophical spirit. This type of work, which already evades any classification within the strict order of university disciplines, makes things even more difficult for itself by taking as the objects of its study phenomena that philosophy does not generally hold in very high esteem: fashion, everyday life, luxury, humour, advertising, consumption. By dignifying the shadows in Plato's cave, the 'electron' seems perhaps to be taking too much of a liberty with the ideal of an ascending dialectic . . .

But I prefer to look at the question from another point of view. The social and historic situation in which we find ourselves is unprecedented: modernity no longer has any invincible enemies, and it has reconciled itself with its principles and its basic values. Thus, the struggles through which modern values imposed themselves (secularism, liberty, equality, democratic pluralism, de-traditionalization) have lost their previous original intensity. Others, to be sure, have taken over their role, but they no longer produce a world intent on breaking away from its past. It follows that the position of intellectuals – who played a major role in the emergence of modernity – can no longer be the same. Today they share the same values as members of society as a whole; they put forward diverging interpretations, but not another collective model. In these conditions, the demand for 'commitment' has diminished: what matters is less taking up the cudgels in defence of this or that, and more understanding a bit better 'how things work' in reality itself. It is of course imperative to problematize moral questions, to raise questions about what is just and unjust, about individual and collective rights, the principle of tolerance, the foundations of liberal society, the legitimacy of different inequalities, etc. But it is no less imperative to examine the workings of society, the way things are actually going and people's real behaviour, in particular when all this provokes the most peremptory and most consensual judgements. If the knowledge of what *is* does not determine what *should be*, it can at least contribute to moving beyond certain sterile and conventional polemics by making sure that people know what they are talking about. It seems to me that by putting forward less stereotypical interpretative models, ones which are less Manichean and more complex, I am participating, in my own modest way, in the debates that the democratic *polis* requires.

As for the polemics in which I have found myself 'embarked', I must say that they have often disappointed me and contributed little to my 'evolution', being too often caricatures, sometimes even shot through with bad faith: this was in particular the case of the harsh critiques launched against *Empire of Fashion* and *La Troisième Femme*. Often the objections are already known in advance, too imprisoned within rigid and invariant models. On the other hand, social and historical change is to a great extent unforeseeable. This is the reason why the confrontation that really interests me, the one that provokes me and makes me develop, is the one which arises from the collision between the facts themselves, in all their complexity, their diversity and their variability. More broadly, I like writing about what I observe rather than writing books about other books.

Let's turn now to your own career. What about your intellectual development and your education? Who were your masters?

I studied philosophy at the Sorbonne in a cultural and intellectual climate quite different from that which prevails these days. At the time, a certain number of us made it a point of honour not to go to lectures, and to take an interest in anything and everything except the university syllabus. The living spirit of philosophy was 'elsewhere': we denounced the mandarins, the dry-as-dust, old-fashioned lectures, the poverty of philosophy. And I read without much passion the founding texts of philosophy. It was somewhat like a free 'artist' making his own decisions about the authors to work on that I pursued my studies. I read with enthusiasm Lévi-Strauss, Saussure, Freud, Marx and his epigones. It wasn't the big questions of metaphysics and ethics that stirred me, but the interpretation of the modern world. Like many students in the Sixties I was imbued with Marxism. Around 1965 I was part of a 'leftist' splinter-group called 'Pouvoir ouvrier' ['Workers' Power'] that sprang from 'Socialisme ou barbarie' ['Socialism or Barbarity'] founded by Lefort and Castoriadis and run in particular by Lyotard, Vega and Souyri. The group proclaimed that it was Marxist-revolutionary: it denounced capitalism and bureaucratic society in both the East and the West. The Soviet Union was seen not as a perverted socialism but as a new society of class exploitation. So the revolution could no longer coincide with the abolition of the private ownership of the means of production: it implied the disappearance of the division between leaders and led, self-management, and the democracy of workers' councils. I stayed in this group for two years, but as I kept going off on holiday, they started to question my mil-

itancy, which seemed a bit too hedonistic and easy-going!
... The new age of leisure was already making its mark ...
I left without any personal crisis, without a bad conscience,
without getting torn up about it. 'True life' for me was
already elsewhere. In fact, the question of the revolution
wasn't particularly an issue for me, and I didn't really believe
in it: what I was looking for above all were tools of analysis
to understand reality. And the lectures provided by the Sorbonne didn't meet my expectations in this regard.

And what was your experience of May 1968?

I enjoyed those spring days, with their interminable and fiery
discussions. I was much less keen on the violence: I didn't
take any part in it. But I never really believed in any truly
revolutionary possibility: people's thoughts seemed to me far
removed from the ideal of the 'great revolution'. In addition,
I had this Marxist idea that 'there can be no revolution
without a revolutionary party', and in May it was impossible
to find any such organization. I couldn't really understand
what was at stake. Paradoxically, it was only a little later that
it all became a bit clearer, when I started focusing on the
question of individualism and the transformations of culture,
values and lifestyles. At the time I experienced those days
with an 'aesthetic' or playful pleasure and a lack of political
awareness. In the end, the most important things happened
in the following years, with the emancipation of personal life,
the way that May 1968 impacted on couples, militancy and
one's relation to politics. The Seventies were throughout
marked by the culture or 'style' of 1968 and its libertarian
ideal, the intensification of personal life. It was in this context
that I read, not without jubilation, Nietzsche, Deleuze and
(Henry) Miller.

And how did your relationship to Marxism develop?

I was never a Communist, Trotskyist or Maoist. It was in
the same line as Castoriadis that I placed myself. In the Sev-

enties, the texts of Lyotard and Baudrillard greatly influenced me: they allowed me, albeit in a radical or avant-garde perspective, to shake off an 'anonymous', Althusserian Marxism, with its structuralist-scientific pretentions, too far removed as it was from the realities of everyday life. Those analyses of desire and pleasure, of consumption and the media, had the merit of subverting separate theoretical domains and revitalizing the critique of the political or libidinal economy, opening up to a realm beyond the political by composing hymns to a 'transpolitical' revolution. From that period on, I considered that everyday existential concerns, lifestyles, everything frivolous, needed to be taken into account and not viewed right from the start as 'false consciousness'. That's why the notion of alienation soon started to irritate me: it expressed too much the idea that people were mystified, passive, manipulated, hypnotized (Debord), incapable of critical distance and of understanding what happens to them. I tried to show in *L'Ère du vide* that things were more complex, that the seductive logic of merchandise was a power capable not merely of deceiving and dispossessing the individual but also of emancipating him. My unease *vis-à-vis* the Marxist analysis can also be explained by what I was reading at the time (Tocqueville, Marcel Gauchet, Louis Dumont, Daniel Bell). In their work, I found some fundamental, indeed irreplaceable models of analysis and tools of conceptualization, that gave back a real productive role to 'ideas' in history: the individual, the democratic revolution, human rights – these were not simply superstructure, a mere 'reflection' of the economy. Then these questions gave me a greater freedom in explaining a new society in which we could see an upsurge of individual autonomy and a lessening of people's subjection to collective frameworks. My analyses of democratic individualism (and not bourgeois individualism, in the Marxist sense) emerged from a combination of several factors: my observation of the revolution in contemporary lifestyles, the rise of a society of consumption and communication, together with the rise of cultural liberalism, American sociology, and analyses derived from the work of Tocqueville.

It's at this point that the notion of postmodernity emerges in your work . . .

I did indeed take up that notion, but in a very pragmatic way, not at all theoretical, let alone philosophical – merely as a tool allowing me to designate a break, a historical *aggiornamento* in the way modern societies function. Lyotard defined the postmodern as a crisis in foundations and the decline in the great systems of legitimation. That was of course correct, but not absolutely so, since democracies in particular rest on a very strong consensus about their main principles and foundations. Then it was necessary to show that there was not just scepticism, incredulity and a loss of belief, but also new landmarks, new reference points and lifestyles. 'Postmodern' to my mind thus implied discontinuity and continuity, a stage that was of course post-revolutionary, post-disciplinary, post-authoritarian, but also one that fitted into the prolongation of the age-old logic of democracy and individualism: hence the idea of a 'second individualist revolution'.

What effect did the success of L'Ère du vide *have on you?*

I remember that when I got my first royalties I treated myself to a wind-surfing board! It wasn't exactly 'changing life' in the way Rimbaud envisaged . . . New intellectual bonds formed that sometimes turned into faithful friendships. I was increasingly asked by the media to analyse the realities of the contemporary world. Especially after *Empire of Fashion*, I was invited more and more often to lecture in France and pretty much everywhere abroad, in universities and in businesses too. Indeed, that was how I managed to get interested in new questions such as luxury or business ethics, questions which my initial education had not prepared me for. The 'void' [of his work *L'Ère du vide* = *The Era of the Void*] thus contributed to keeping my days very full and increasing the amount of contact I had with the world – it enabled me better to embrace the plenitude of reality!

Your love of facts leads you to emphasize the descriptive more than the normative and not to put forward any new norms. How do you explain this neglect when it is a question of tackling the examination of possible solutions?

As a citizen, I may have commitments to make and decisions to take, but I don't want to mix genres. What interests me in my work is understanding the different kinds of logic operating in history and modernity and not judging them. In any case, judging can be a tricky business. For example, concerning the question I raise in *Le Luxe éternel*, it would have been easy to relapse into condemnation or praise. But if you accept the analysis put forward, showing that luxury cannot just be seen reductively as that which is superfluous, and that it is consubstantial with the history of the human race, then the question of the normative soon becomes an empty question. Are we going to start condemning the age-old offerings to the gods and the erection of lavish temples? That's absurd. It is vain to seek to judge something that is constitutive of the social and human domain.

Sure, but can't we pass judgement not on the history of luxury but on luxury as it exists these days?

Of course, that's altogether possible, but it's not such an easy business as people think. On the one hand, luxury undeniably has something shocking about it. But on the other, who really wishes for a purely functional society, without dreams, without wastage, without prestigious mythologies and superlative forms? Don't we quite legitimately long for the most beautiful things? If we say that luxury is 'bad', where do we draw the line? It's an old question: where does the 'superfluous' begin? When does luxury start to become unacceptable? And what is a 'real' need? Is art a form of luxury? If so, what should we do with it? Here we embark on a type of debate where the arguments don't manage to carry conviction, where they are more a matter of rationalizing emotional reactions than expressing a real attempt to know. I'll leave such arguments to others. They really don't interest me very much. Above all, I think that there's no possibility of giving a definite, properly justified answer to that question.

Do you also think that, concerning fashion, judgements are just as cut-and-dried as they are for luxury?

Of course. People are forever denouncing the mimicry inherent in mass crazes, the superficiality of the telly, the triviality of consumption. Not without excellent reasons, at times. And yet fashion, as I analysed it in *Empire of Fashion* allows a less Manichean approach to the phenomenon. After all, the society of fashion (that of consumption, the media, advertising, the 'disposable' object) is also the society that has forced bloodthirsty forms of fanaticism to retreat, reinforced the legitimacy of democratic pluralism, and enabled a greater liberty of public opinion and more freedom for electors. Even if its many negative effects are real, its benefits are very far from being null and void. I merely wished to show that fashion as a form didn't spell 'barbarity', and wasn't a disaster for thought and freedom. The question deserves a more attentive examination and more nuanced judgements than are often to be found in the works written by the 'professionals' of the concept and other finicky interpreters of the great canonic texts.

A rereading of L'Ère du vide *can create the impression that the big concepts that run though your work are already in place: the process of personalization, the destruction of the collective structures of meaning, the value accorded to hedonism, the revolution of consumption, paradoxical tensions within civil society and individuals themselves, the importance of seduction as a mode of social regulation, the pacification of the political, and a deeper attachment to the essential values of democracy. And yet, we are no longer within a postmodern context. So what has changed structurally since 1983, the date of publication of your first book?*

Many 'things' have changed: the rise of globalization and the market society, the consecration of human rights, new forms of poverty and social exclusion, the casualization of labour, the increasing fears and anxieties of every sort, the establishment of the National Front in the political landscape. But also, the end of an international system dominated by East–West antagonism, the explosion of new conflicts and wars of identity. Many of these changes may contradict the idea I was putting forward: namely, the advent of a less 'tensed up' society and a 'cool' individual. In fact, I'm busy right now trying to X-ray, as it were, certain aspects of this new context. Does it mean that nothing remains of the revolution in the new individualism? Obviously not. For these reasons (in no particular order): hedonism is no longer so joyfully triumphant, but all the same it governs a whole set of mass practices. Individual autonomy appears increasingly as a norm imposed by organizations, but the life of choice, the do-it-yourself life, continues. The constraints of professional life are being reinforced, and the volatility of electors, couples, consumers and believers is becoming greater. The successes of the National Front may pose a problem for the idea of an open, tolerant individualism. And yet, on the other hand, the phenomenon illustrates in its way the thesis of the democratic consolidation entailed by the society of fashion and its individualism. The extreme Right has not assumed power; society as a whole has not succumbed to the temptation of xenophobia and nationalism; the government, although right-wing, has not made a pact with Le Pen. The dynamics of individualization have led to democracy remaining solid, attached to its humanistic and pluralistic principles.

The climate has changed, but the fact remains that the hyper-modern individual, whether hedonist or anxious, is none the less far from nihilist. Duty is no longer unconditional, morality is no longer authoritarian, commitment is no longer absolute, and yet we are not in a society that is lacking in all values. How do you explain this?

Tocqueville as well as Durkheim emphasized that a society cannot be reduced to material production and economic exchanges. It cannot exist without ideal conceptions. These are not a 'luxury' which it can do without, but the very condition of collective existence, a fact which enables individuals to be attached to one another, to have common goals and to act together. Without a system of values there is no social body capable of reproducing itself. Hypermodern society does not escape this law. Far from having caused the annihilation of all values, the débâcle of the great political messianic dreams has enabled democracies to become reconciled to their basic moral principles: human rights. On the one side, individualism leads to a decline in the strength of moral obligations; on the other, it contributes to giving to the latter a new priority. Respect for the person could appear secondary when it was compared with revolution, class struggle, the nation, or even the race. This is no longer the case. We need to stop singing the old refrain that we live in a nihilistic, anarchic universe, delivered from all moral meaning, all belief in good and evil: the decadence of values is a myth, and one that, incidentally, is far from new. In addition, on another level, we need to remember the fact that the dynamic of individualism reinforces the tendency to identification with the other. Tocqueville thus spoke of a 'general compassion for all members of the human race'. As an effect of the imaginary idea of equality and the cult of well-being, individuals are more deeply 'touched' by the spectacle of the sufferings of another: this underlies the different reactions of indignation, the rise of an ethics of sentiment exploited by the media, the new forms of altruism and generosity, which, even if they are not 'obligatory', are none the less real.

So we have individuals who are coming closer and closer to one another, an equality that is being achieved, and ontological differences that persist, notably between men and women. At the very moment when the process of increasing equality might have led to an increasingly evident androgyny, we observe that sexual differentiation remains, as if there were an eternal feminine. The

*feminists, as we know, attribute such a survival to an archaic
heritage that is bound to disappear. This may appear plausible
but, none the less, you are not convinced. Why not?*

For two fundamental reasons. First, what is being perpetuated does not exclude the principle of the free individual
governance of women. Not all the social codes inherited from
the past persist: virginity, or the ideal of the housewife, have
collapsed, even in spite of their previous social power. If
other norms and roles, on the contrary, are being maintained,
this is because they are now compatible with the principle
of personal autonomy. As a result, the new permanent ideal
of the feminine does not appear as a pure 'survival', but as a
reinvention of tradition by women, a recycling of the past in
the free order of individualist modernity. Beauty, for instance,
remains a norm assigned primarily to women, but this norm
no longer prevents them from studying, working or assuming political responsibilities. The same is true of the still pre-
ponderant place occupied by women in the domestic space.
Doubtless they often complain of their husbands' 'absence':
the fact remains that if this traditional role is being played
again, it is no longer synonymous with being trapped within
the family and with the denial of their right to do what they
want with their lives.

The second reason is just as important. I don't think that
a society can fail to find a symbolic translation for sexual difference. How can we imagine human beings not giving some
social meaning to sexual difference? It seems to me that what
we have here is, as it were, an anthropological and cognitive
imperative. Let's take a frivolous example. In the Sixties,
radical feminists burned their bras, which were in their view
a symbol of the way women were treated as objects. What's
the situation today? Underwear has never been so eroticized.
How is such a phenomenon to be explained? Is it a 'regression'? I don't think so. With the feminization of education
and employment, with the destabilization of roles and the
way that women have managed to reach posts of responsibility that used to be a masculine preserve, there is a growing

need to reassert feminine identity by subtle but evident signs. As the great monolithic divisions between the genders are reduced, we see the demand for something like a universe of sexual difference to be given shape. I can assure you that the age of equality does not lead to a confluence of genders, to an androgynous erasure of the distinction between masculine and feminine roles.

Let's turn to your current work, which questions our present situation from the standpoint of an analysis based on such different factors as luxury, the cult of the present, or the way the market dominates everything in the world in an era of emotional consumption. In all three cases, one and the same process is at work, emphasizing the importance of hedonism and emotions – an emphasis which can be explained by the new equality of opportunity, and by individualism and de-institutionalization taken to their logical conclusion. This expresses a new relationship to objects, to others and to oneself – a relationship which consumption, perhaps, brings out very clearly. Can you say a word or two about that?

What I call the society of hyperconsumption is the society which sees an erosion of the old frameworks of class and the appearance of a volatile, fragmentary and deregulated consumer. At the same time, we are witnessing the sudden rise of a consumption that is much more experiential or emotional than statutory. We consume much more for ourselves (health, relaxation, fitness, sensations, travel) in order to gain recognition from the other. Look at the big and ever-growing sectors of consumption such as health. I wish the best of luck to anyone who tries to explain medical overconsumption by drawing on the model of 'distinction'! The logic of prestige still plays an important role, of course, but it is merely part of a much broader picture and cannot be the final reason behind the escalation in consumerism. What people are looking for, above all, in consumption these days is a feeling, an intense emotional pleasure, which is dependent less on their status than on the very experience of the pleasure of novelty. Through 'things', what is being expressed, in the final analysis, is a new relationship to personal existence, just as if people were afraid of getting bogged down, of not being ceaselessly provided with new sensations. They're terrorized by the boredom of repetition, by the way that their intimate experiences soon 'age'. To buy something means we're playing the game – buying a touch of novelty in our subjective daily lives. Here, perhaps, lies the ultimate meaning of the mechanism of hyperconsumption.

So modernity is an emotional hyperconsumption – in other words, a consumption that is no longer imagined on the basis of a symbolic confrontation whose aim is social distinction, but as the possibility of giving new birth to oneself in pleasure, not pain. And that modernity has reached its end, leaving us to grapple with the ideal figure of modern man, free and equal to others – the figure of the hyperconsumer. Does hypermodernity condemn us to the triumph of market forces throughout the world? And what threats lurk in the process?

What characterizes hyperconsumption or globalized consumption is the fact that even the non-economic sphere (family, religion, trades unionism, education, procreation, ethics) is invaded by the mentality of consumer man. However, this cosmos does not mean the elimination of non-market values, of feelings, or of altruism. The more the commercialization of life imposes itself, the more we celebrate human rights. At the same time, voluntary work, love and friendship are values that perpetuate and even reinforce themselves. Even if exchanges with a price label attached are becoming the rule, our affective sentimental, empathetic humanity is not being threatened. It's an old idea: Marx was already saying that the bourgeoisie had replaced all the old ties of affection by money – at the very moment when the family was being most overtly idealized and romantic love was at its height. In fact, the modern consecration of merchandise occurred in tandem with the development of intimacy, with love marriages and an investment of affection in the child.

The dangers lie elsewhere. In particular, we are seeing a worrying trend towards a greater fragility and emotional instability on the part of individuals. Hyperconsumption dismantled all the forms of socialization that used to provide individuals with points of reference. Durkheim had already emphasized this: it is not because a society becomes harsher that there is an epidemic of suicides; it is because individuals are thrown back on their own resources and thereby are less well prepared to face up to the miseries of existence. Today, if individuals are more and more fragile, this is less because the cult of performance is destroying them than because the great social institutions no longer provide individuals with any solid structural frame. Hence the spiralling number of psychosomatic disorders, depressions and other anxieties that are the other face of the society of happiness. If this observation is correct, it means that the search for happiness highlighted by the moderns is very far from having been achieved. Material well-being is on the increase, consumption is shooting up, but *joie de vivre* does not follow the same rhythm, as the hypermodern individual loses in ease of living what he gains in operational speed, in comfort, in a longer life-span.

And what happens to philosophy in this hypermodern world? How can it play its role of being a rational discourse in the face of individuals more inclined to reacting emotionally than to thinking things through?

Let me remind you, first, that hypermodernity cannot be reduced to an all-pervasive consumerism, distraction and channel-hopping. It has not, in fact, abolished the will to surpass oneself, to create, to invent, to seek, to defy the difficulties of life and thought. Even with the contemporary consumer-in-overdrive, the 'will to power' never ceases to be active. As a result, philosophy as a discipline of reason and a quest for truth is not under threat. There is no reason why we should witness a disappearance of all people who nurse the ambition of rising above prejudices and embarking on the difficult tasks of grasping the world in concepts. But neither is there any reason to think that such an attitude can spread to the wider audience. On the other hand, what does have every chance of spreading is the mass consumption of certain works either of the 'philosophy for beginners' type or of 'meditations' aiming at promoting happiness. In a period of individualist do-it-yourself, Seneca and Montaigne make an appearance in the domain of consumption next to Prozac – a whole public goes to philosophy for consolation, for empirical and immediate recipes for happiness. Good luck to the hyperconsumer – but it's difficult for me not to express my greatest scepticism, as this type of reading produces everything but the hoped-for effect: philosophy is not the royal road to bliss. Reading great works may indeed arouse wonder, fill you with enthusiasm, give you a certain limited satisfaction here and there: this is better than nothing, but it doesn't go very far towards bringing you closer to a happy life. Someone who has meditated on the great masters is no better prepared for happiness than anyone else, and no philosopher can protect you from the experience of sadness, despair, pain or fear. In this respect I feel Hegelian: philosophy's task is to make reality intelligible and nothing more; its role is to shed a little light, not to give us the keys to happiness, which, as is quite obvious, nobody holds.

Another point. The importance of the role that philosophy has played in the history of ideas, culture, rationality and modernity no longer needs to be demonstrated. It invented the great metaphysical questionings, the idea of a cosmopolitan humanity, the value of individuality and freedom; it nourished for centuries the work of artists, poets and writers; it contributed to forging the principles of the democratic life; it dreamt of changing the social, political and economic world. Today that age-old force has exhausted itself. There is of course no lack of works of high quality, but they no longer succeed in imbuing the thoughts of artists and writers apart from 'professional' philosophers themselves. It's a sign of the times: there are no more 'isms', no more great philosophical schools. We are obliged to recognize that its historical and

'Promethean' role is behind us. It is the sciences and technology that now open the most perspectives, invent the
future, change the present and life itself, inspire creative
thinkers. The whole Renaissance fed on ancient wisdom, and
until the eighteenth century, Stoicism, Epicureanism and
Pyrrhonism exerted a major influence on people's minds. I
do not feel that what we are creating in the philosophical
domain can enjoy an analogous destiny. Philosophy may be
fashionable, but we will never return to the *status quo*, and
nothing will arrest the process that is reducing its influence
on the life of culture. On the one hand, we have a democratization of access to the major works; on the other, a philosophical space that is increasingly concentrated on the
institution of the university. On the one hand, works read by
a tiny number of scholars or indeed by nobody; on the other,
immense best-sellers whose influence is increasingly a matter
of pure consumption, short-lived and only skin-deep, since
philosophy can no longer escape the pre-eminence of the
logic of the ephemeral. These various scenarios of the fate of
philosophy in the era of hypermodernism are neither doom-
laden nor particularly inspiring.

BIBLIOGRAPHY OF PUBLICATIONS BY GILLES LIPOVETSKY

BOOKS

L'Ère du vide: essais sur l'individualisme contemporain (Paris: Gallimard, 1983; republished in collection 'Folio Essais').

L'Empire de l'éphémère: la mode et son destin dans les sociétés modernes (Paris: Gallimard, 1987; republished in collection 'Folio Essais'); English version: *The Empire of Fashion: Dressing Modern Democracy*, tr. Catherine Porter (Princeton: Princeton University Press, 1994).

Le Crépuscule du devoir: l'éthique indolore des nouveaux temps démocratiques (Paris: Gallimard, 1992; republished in collection 'Folio Essais').

La Troisième Femme: permanence et révolution du féminin (Paris: Gallimard, 1997).

Métamorphoses de la culture libérale: ethique, médias, enterprise (Montreal: Liber, 2002).

Le Luxe éternel: de l'âge du sacré aux temps des marques, with Elyette Roux (Paris: Gallimard, 2003).

ARTICLES (THOSE MARKED WITH AN ASTERISK HAVE BEEN PUBLISHED IN BOOKS)

'Travail, désir', *Critique*, 314 (1973).

'Fragments énergétiques à propos du capitalisme', *Critique* 335 (1975).

'Pouvoir de la répétition', *L'Arc*, 64 (1976).

'Mise en scène du temps', *Silex*, 4 (1977).

'Dissémination de la terreur', *Silex*, 10 (1978).

'Jeux d'organes' (on Michel Lablais), with Michel Dupart, *Silex*, 10 (1978).

'Sans issue' (on Peter Klasen), *Silex*, 10 (1978).

*'Séduction non stop', *Traverses*, 17 (1979).

*'L'indifférence pure', *Traverses*, 19 (1980).

'Monument interdit', *Le débat*, 4 (1980).

*'Narcisse ou la stratégie du vide', *Le débat*, 5 (1980).

*'La société humoristique', *Le débat*, 5 (1980).

'L'art moderne et l'individualisme démocratique', *Le débat*, 21 (1982).

*'La mode de cent ans', *Le débat*, 31 (1984).

'Changer la vie ou l'irruption de l'individualisme transpolitique', *Pouvoirs*, 39 (1986), tr. as May '68 or The rise of transpolitical individualism', in Mark Lilla (ed.), *New French Thought: Political Philosophy* (Princeton: Princeton University Press, 1994).

*'La pub sort ses griffes', *Le débat*, 43 (1987).

'Un mystique de la peau' (on Horst Egon Kalinowksi), *Cimaise*, 202 (1989).

'Virage culturel, persistence du moi', *Le débat*, 60 (1990).

'Sergio Ferro ou les dessus et les dessous de la peinture', in Sergio Ferro, *Editions de l'Entrée des artistes* (1990).

'Espace privé, espace public à l'âge postmoderne', in *Citoyenneté et urbanité* (Paris: Edition Esprit, 1991).

'Art et publicité: vers l'accessoirisation de la vie?', Catalogue of the exhibition *Art et publicité*, Centre Georges-Pompidou, 1991.

*'Les noces de l'éthique et du business', *Le débat*, 67 (1991).

'High and low: les intellectuels et les valeurs culturelles dans la France d'aujourd'hui', in *The Florence Gould Lectures*, New York University, 1990–1992.

'Fashion and neo-intellectualism', *International Textiles*, 740 (1993).

'Eclipse de la distance, morale de l'urgence', in *La recherche photographique*, 15 (1993).

'Le marketing en quête d'âme', *Revue française de marketing*, 153–4 (1995).

'La balkanisation de la mode: liberté et anxiété des apparences', *L'esprit créateur*, University of Kentucky, 37(1) (1997).

'La femme réinventée', *Le débat*, 100 (1998).

'La mujer y la actividad profesional', in *Dimensiones economicas y sociales de la familia* (Madrid: Visor, 2000).

'The contribution of mass media', *Ethical Perspectives*, 7 (2–3) (2000).

'La revolución de lo femenino', in *Educar en la ciudadania*, (Valencia, Instituticó Alfons el Magnanim, 2001).

'More than fashion', in *Chic Clicks, Commerce and Creativity in Contemporary Fashion Photography* (Boston: The Institute of Contemporary Art, 2002).

'La société d'hyperconsommation', *Le débat*, 124 (2003).